MW01070672

Early Praise for
No Substitute for Victory

"In *No Substitute for Victory*, Theodore and Donna Kinni have captured the essence of the extraordinary leadership skills and strategic vision of General Douglas MacArthur with whom I was privileged to serve in Tokyo and in the early months of the Korean War, including the landings at Inchon. MacArthur epitomized 'Duty, Honor, Country,' and he will ever be a 'role model' for our nation's leaders—in and out of uniform."

—General Alexander M. Haig, Jr.,
Former NATO Commander and U.S. Secretary of State

"A first-rate, and inspirational, look at how leaders make a difference. While MacArthur may have been 'one of a kind,' we can all benefit from learning about the leadership processes and insights he brought to bear on both grand and individual issues. *No Substitute for Victory* is an up-close and personal look at MacArthur and how he thought about and demonstrated leadership. Full of provocative and thoughtful insights, the book will encourage each of us to reflect on our own leadership opportunities."

—Barry Posner, Ph.D., Co-author: *The Leadership Challenge and Credibility*, and International Management Council's Management/Leadership Educator of the Year

"We now know that leaders of all types can learn a lot from military leaders, but Douglas MacArthur has largely been overlooked in this regard. Every senior executive can profit from reading about this intense but thoughtful general, and the lessons in this book are well-structured and easily accessed."

—Thomas H. Davenport, President's Distinguished Professor, Babson College, Accenture Fellow

"For those aspiring to be successful national leaders, CEOs, military commanders, diplomats, educators, think-tankers, and all others whose career ambitions involve commitment to public service, *No Substitute for Victory* is a must-read book. This clear and pure distillation of the life and times of General Douglas MacArthur by the Kinni team holds precious lessons for all who care, share, and dare in order to make a difference. Vision resulting in fulfillment is most likely to happen through the exercise of resolute leadership of the MacArthur kind."

—Fidel V. Ramos, Former President of the Philippines

"The Kinnis have probed the remarkable life of Douglas MacArthur to great advantage, proving once again that great military leadership offers invaluable lessons for the corporate world. While several of these are lessons we seem to have to keep re-learning, many of their insights shed new light on the challenge of leadership, not only at the highest levels, but throughout the organization."

—Jon R. Katzenbach, Senior Partner—Katzenbach Partners LLC, and author of *Peak Performance* and *Why Pride Matters More Than Money*

"General Douglas MacArthur was a genuine American hero who has inspired generations of military men and women. Theodore and Donna Kinni's analysis of MacArthur's gifts as a leader will help the readers develop those talents in everyday life. While MacArthur's lessons will be of particular interest to those in uniform, this book offers practical advice to all those wishing to improve their leadership skills."

—Congressman Ike Skelton, Ranking Democrat on the House Armed Services Committee

"By distilling General MacArthur's extraordinary approach to leadership into distinct lessons, Theodore and Donna Kinni have performed a valuable service. In this honest and engaging book, the authors demonstrate the importance of values, vision, and proficiency in the General's leadership style. They challenge us, with a series of thought-provoking questions in each chapter, to learn from and to follow his example."

—John Alexander, President, Center for Creative Leadership

"Drawing leadership lessons from military heroes is often hard to do simply because the human being is lost somewhere in the uniform, the brigades, and the battles. The Kinnis, however, have brought General MacArthur to life—not just as a soldier but as a person struggling to live by taking his own highest principles and bringing them to life. There's no doubt that we can learn from MacArthur's career, and his life is vividly portrayed in this short, poignant, and most powerful book."

—Tom Brown, author of *The Anatomy of Fire: Sparking a New Spirit of Enterprise* (Foreword by Jim Collins) and keynote essayist for *Business, The Ultimate Resource*

"Theodore and Donna Kinni have written a masterful work that superbly distilled the leadership lessons from the extraordinary career of one of America's greatest leaders. The depth, complexity, and brilliance of General MacArthur's leadership are brought out in crisp lessons for all leaders to draw and reflect upon. This is an essential, must read addition to any leadership library."

—General Anthony C. Zinni, USMC United States Marine Corps (Retired)

"An extraordinary book about an extraordinary leader. Everyone can learn from following MacArthur, a strategic genius, and *No Substitute for Victory* maps the way."

—W.E.B. Griffin, Author of over 33 books, including *By Order Of The President, Under Fire,* and *Retreat, Hell!*

"In 1978, William Manchester published American Caesar, the magisterial warts-and-all portrait of Douglas MacArthur the man. Now Theodore and Donna Kinni have brought us an important portrait of MacArthur the leader and strategist. Here is a study of the very mechanisms and methods that made Mac the architect of victory in the Pacific during World War II and that culminated in the assault on Inchon during the Korean War, a strategic and tactical masterpiece on a par with Hannibal's Cannae. A common sense, fascinating, and eminently practical book, *No Substitute for Victory* is not aimed at the military specialist, but at CEOs, managers, supervisors, and everyone else whose job it is to lead people in a common enterprise."

—Alan Axelrod, author of *Patton on Leadership: Strategic Lessons for Corporate Warfare* and *Office Superman: Make Yourself Indispensable in the Workplace*

"Here, Ted and Donna Kinni capture the essential MacArthur—a controversial general sometimes, but a remarkable leader always. His strategic decisions have down-to-earth pertinence to corporate 'wars.'"

—Al Vogl, Editor, *Across the Board, The Conference Board Magazine*

"The life of Douglas MacArthur is too often reduced to a few familiar milestones, and not all of them positive! The general's battle with Truman, and his eventual dismissal, is, after all, a case study in how not to manage up. Pushing beyond these iconic episodes, however, Theodore and Donna Kinni reveal the scores of small and large events, actions, decisions, and testimonials from MacArthur's life story that show why this complex, driven soldier is a brilliant model for the 50 hard-hitting leadership lessons contained in these pages."

—Chris Murray, Editor in Chief, *Soundview Executive Book Summaries*

"Are the statements and actions of a leader in a certain place and time relevant signposts to others in radically different contexts? The Kinnis' answer is a resounding 'Yes.' Their creative use of synoptic highlights of General MacArthur's ideas and behaviors present thought-provoking material for would-be leaders in the 21st century."

—Blythe J. McGarvie, President, Leadership for International Finance and former director on several corporate boards, including Accenture, Wawa, and The Pepsi Bottling Group

NO SUBSTITUTE *for* VICTORY

LESSONS IN STRATEGY AND LEADERSHIP FROM GENERAL DOUGLAS MACARTHUR

NO SUBSTITUTE *for* VICTORY

LESSONS IN STRATEGY AND LEADERSHIP FROM GENERAL DOUGLAS MACARTHUR

With Best Regards,

By Theodore Kinni and Donna Kinni

An Imprint of PEARSON EDUCATION
Upper Saddle River, NJ • New York • London • San Francisco • Toronto • Sydney
Tokyo • Singapore • Hong Kong • Cape Town • Madrid
Paris • Milan • Munich • Amsterdam

www.ft-ph.com

Library of Congress Number: 2004110317

Publisher: *Tim Moore*
Acquisitions Editor: *Paula Sinnott*
Editorial Assistant: *Richard Winkler*
Development Editor: *Russ Hall*
Marketing Manager: *Martin Litkowski*
International Marketing Manager: *Tim Galligan*
Cover Designer: *Chuti Prasertsith*
Managing Editor: *Gina Kanouse*
Production: *Specialized Composition, Inc.*
Manufacturing Buyer: *Dan Uhrig*

Pearson Education, Inc.
Publishing as Financial Times Prentice Hall
Upper Saddle River, New Jersey 07458

Printed in the United States of America

First Printing: January, 2005

ISBN: 0-13-147021-3

Pearson Education LTD.
Pearson Education Australia PTY, Limited.
Pearson Education Singapore, Pte. Ltd.
Pearson Education North Asia, Ltd.
Pearson Education Canada, Ltd.
Pearson Educatión de Mexico, S.A. de C.V.
Pearson Education—Japan

For Ada and her husbands:

Frank J. Cumiskey, a lifelong advocate of athletics, who competed in gymnastics on the U.S. Olympic Team a record 16 years from 1932 to 1948 and founded the National Gymnastics Judges Association.

Gordon Hutcheon, a visionary leader, who served as mayor and councilman of Rockleigh, NJ for 40 years and was instrumental in the successful preservation and development of the town.

Contents

Authors' Acknowledgements

The beginning is usually the best place to start, so we must first thank Geoff Thatcher, then Creative Director at the Tom Peters Company, now at Carat Brand Experience, who planted the seed that grew into this book. Geoff's enthusiastic description of MacArthur's achievements and, producers take note, his riveting screenplay based on MacArthur's experiences in WWI compelled us to examine the General's life for lessons for leaders.

Bill Davis, Director of The General Douglas MacArthur Foundation and Executive Director of The MacArthur Memorial, heard us out and lent his considerable support to the book. His interest and cooperation were and continue to be instrumental in the success of this project. Likewise Jim Zoebel, the Memorial's archivist, was unstintingly generous with his time and knowledge, as well as access to the Archive's rich primary source materials. We hope that their efforts will be repaid many times.

Financial Times Prentice Hall publisher Tim Moore recognized MacArthur as a genuine American hero and clearly saw the relevance for today's leaders. Acquisitions editor Paula Sinnott jumped in halfway through and kept the book on track with elbow grease and great advice. Chuti Prasertsith hit a home run on the first pitch with the cover design.

Forbes chairman Caspar Weinberger was exceedingly generous both in discussing MacArthur and contributing the book's preface. It is a great honor to be even slightly associated with such a fundamentally decent man and accomplished leader. Thanks also to executive assistant Kay Leisz for her facilitation skills and support.

We thank the book's reviewers and endorsers—John Alexander, Alan Axelrod, Tom Brown, Thomas Davenport, W.E.B. Griffin, Alexander Haig, Jon Katzenbach, Blythe McGarvie, Chris Murray, Barry Posner, Fidel V. Ramos, Ike Skelton, Al Vogl, and Anthony Zinni. They took hours out of their busy schedules to read the galleys and offer their comments. We are awed in the company of such a distinguished group of accomplished leaders and leadership experts. Their support for the book is much appreciated.

Finally, for proofreading services above and beyond the call of duty, thanks to Joan Kinni and Ray Rieman.

Foreword

N*o Substitute for Victory* introduces a new generation of aspiring leaders to General Douglas MacArthur, whose entire career demonstrated the meaning of leadership. The book also demonstrates how vital it was for the nation to have had the benefit of General MacArthur's genius in all of the posts in which he served us so long, so brilliantly, and with such creativity.

Few of today's generation can recall all that MacArthur accomplished, let alone how he did it. So this new biographical study is not only timely, it also serves as a splendid way to learn the strategic and leadership lessons that MacArthur provided us.

No Substitute for Victory is far more than a standard biography. It contains descriptions, short and concise, that convey the astonishing dimensions of the General's career from the beginnings of his military training, before his years as a cadet at West Point, and beyond, including: his combat service during World War I; his reorganization of West Point as its superintendent and then, the entire Army during his Chief of Staff years; his service to the Philippines, forming, training, and leading their military; and of course, the many-pronged ways in which he helped win World War II in the Pacific and sealed that victory later in Japan and Korea.

After all military operations, "lessons learned" sessions are held in Washington. Some of the most valuable parts of this book, the various leadership principles that guided the General's actions and the strategies he used throughout his long and productive career, are comparable to those studies.

From the military point of view, perhaps MacArthur's greatest wartime strategy was his decision to avoid costly frontal attacks against Japanese-held islands and instead, simply going above and around them. This lesson is presented here fully and skillfully. In the chapter titled "The Principles of Occupation," there is a list of five principles of management based on one of MacArthur's greatest accomplishments, the occupation and reform of Japan. The foundation for MacArthur's success in Japan stemmed to a great extent from his decision to retain the Emperor. Thus, was he able to secure the support, and later, the virtual adoration, of the Japanese people even as they experienced the traumatic changes they had to undertake in the aftermath of the war.

The importance of courage is also well illustrated. Of General MacArthur's personal bravery there can never be any question. One of my favorite examples is the General's decision to go, virtually alone, to Japan after the surrender. He went unarmed and in a single plane to what was left of Atsugi Airport accompanied by only a small number of his personal staff. For the two hours it took to reach Yokohama, MacArthur was driven past hundreds of thousands of Japan's citizens and the armed soldiers of that conquered nation, who lined the way.

Winston Churchill recalling this said, "Of all the amazing acts of bravery in the war, I regard MacArthur's landing at Atsugi as the greatest of the lot." This was not sheer bravado; by that act MacArthur established both his absolute authority *and* his trust in the Japanese people.

There is, of course, much more to learn in this book for leaders of all ilks. Organizational managers, military officers, and students of leadership alike will find valuable lessons in *No Substitute for Victory*. I would think also that this book should be required reading for West Point cadets.

Caspar W. Weinberger
Chairman, Forbes, Inc.
Secretary of Defense under President Ronald Reagan
November 2004

Introduction

What Leaders Can Learn From MacArthur

I never met General Douglas MacArthur, but it seems like he has always been a presence in my life. As a boy, I was spellbound by my uncle's stories of World War II. He served with the First Cavalry Division during the liberation of the Philippines, and the pride my uncle had in the accomplishments of his unit and its association with the General ran deep below the surface of his well-deserved bravado.

Later, as a history major in college, I studied the operations in the Pacific during World War II and gained a great respect for MacArthur's strategic genius. When I was commissioned in the United States Marine Corps in 1966, I first visited the MacArthur Memorial while attending the Basic School in Quantico, Virginia. It was after my retirement as Deputy Director of the Marine Corps History and Museums, when I became Director of The MacArthur Memorial and Executive Director of The General Douglas MacArthur Foundation, that I came to be immersed in all things MacArthur and gained my greatest appreciation for the man who President Ronald Reagan called "an authentic American hero."

General MacArthur was one of our nation's preeminent military leaders. During World War II, he was one of only five people to earn the grade of General of the Army. The longevity of his military leadership career has rarely been equaled. With the exception of a short interlude just prior to World War II, he served continuously in the United States Army from his plebe year at West Point in 1899 until his recall in 1951.

From 1918 onward, for over 30 years, he was a general officer with ever increasing command responsibilities.

His military accomplishments are just as formidable as his longevity. MacArthur served as an observer or participant in twenty campaigns in six wars. He was a courageous combat leader in World War I, an instrumental figure in the winning of World War II, and the architect of the Amphibious Assault at Inchon—an operation that turned the course of the Korean War. MacArthur was one of our nation's most decorated officers, earning myriad awards from the Medal of Honor to more than 60 foreign decorations. Winston Churchill thought him the best American commander of World War II.

MacArthur was also one of those rare leaders whose abilities transcended his chosen profession. His statesmanship was proven in the Philippines, Australia, and most notably, during his stewardship over the 80 million citizens of postwar Japan, where it can be truly said that he helped win the peace. He proved his administrative abilities as U.S. Army Chief of Staff during the Great Depression and as Superintendent of U.S. Military Academy at West Point in the early 1920s. Many regard him as the father of today's West Point for his efforts to modernize the academy after World War I.

MacArthur's leadership accomplishments did not stop there. He led the U.S. Olympic team to victory in the 1928 Summer Games. And, in the last decade of his life, he became a corporate leader, as chairman of the board at Remington Rand, Inc. and then, Sperry Rand Corp., and a noted spokesperson for American business.

MacArthur's story makes fascinating and dramatic historical reading, but is it relevant to current and aspiring leaders? The answer, as you'll see in the pages to come, is a resounding affirmative. As MacArthur himself believed and demonstrated, history is our greatest teacher. Although the passing of time often renders tactics and technologies ineffective, the underlying principles on which they are based tend to remain sound. That is why I believe that the 50 lessons in strategy and leadership derived from MacArthur's life and career are as important today as they were in the century past.

Before you leap into those lessons, I'd like to offer you three foundational components of successful long-term leadership that are reiterated throughout this book and observed in MacArthur's life and career. They are values, vision, and proficiency.

Great leadership is first and foremost moral leadership. Values are the guideposts by which a leader determines the boundaries of a proper course of action. Repeatedly throughout history, we have seen what happens when sound leadership values are subverted. The most recent example is the financial scandals that followed the economic boom of the late 1990s, when the pursuit of personal reward superceded integrity.

MacArthur's leadership example is one that was securely tethered to values and even 40 years after his death, these values continue to be closely associated with him. They are Duty, Honor, and Country—the West Point credo and the cornerstone of our nation's military leadership.

Duty is the duty to your organization, to those you lead, and to those you follow. Honor is the imperative of personal integrity. Country is the support in word and deed of the principles on which our nation is based. These are values that can provide a firm foundation for the leaders of any organization, and I urge you to adopt and rigorously practice them.

Vision is second component of long-term leadership effectiveness. Successful leaders must be visionaries in order to set a course of action. They must be able to see beyond the daily turmoil and understand the bigger picture. Without a visionary leader, an organization is condemned to forever react.

In this book, you will see how MacArthur was always looking forward—attempting to grasp the challenges looming ahead and formulating strategies capable of overcoming them. Like all great military commanders, he abhorred a passive defense and was always envisioning methods to turn the tide and grasp the offensive. The invasion at Inchon, as you will see in Chapter 1, was a notable example of how a leader's vision can transform a losing proposition into a decisive victory.

The final foundational component of long-term leadership effectiveness is proficiency. Leaders must be highly proficient in order to successfully execute a course of action. They must be lifelong learners and relentless practitioners of their craft. They must hone all of the skills and talents needed to succeed and bring them to bear on whatever tasks they choose to undertake.

The lessons in this book describe many of the skills and talents required of leaders. You will see why they are important and how MacArthur developed and practiced them. You will also get a glimpse into MacArthur's many achievements and see how his success was enabled by concentrated study and hard work. Certainly there are those who are born to lead, and you can make a good case that MacArthur was one of them. But leaders, including MacArthur, will never achieve their full potential unless they build their proficiency.

Values, vision, and proficiency—these are key elements of leadership excellence and organizational victory. It is my hope that General MacArthur's example inspires and assists you in your quest to achieve both. Enjoy the book, come visit the MacArthur Memorial, and thank you for supporting The General Douglas MacArthur Foundation!

William J. Davis, Colonel, USMC (Retired)
Director, The MacArthur Memorial
Executive Director, The General Douglas
MacArthur Foundation
Norfolk, Virginia

☆☆☆☆☆

PART ONE

THE GREAT COMMANDER

Chapter 1

MacArthur at Inchon

General Douglas MacArthur stood at the bow of the *Mount McKinley*, the flagship of Task Force 90, facing the coast of South Korea in the darkness ahead. It was 2:30 a.m. on September 15, 1950. Operation Chromite, MacArthur's audacious amphibious invasion of the port city of Inchon, was scheduled to begin at dawn.

MacArthur's confidence throughout the planning of Chromite, which he had conceived to wrest control of the Korean War and liberate South Korea from the North Korean invaders, had been complete and seemingly unshakable. Yet, in the tense hours before dawn, he obviously felt the full weight of leadership. "Within five hours, 40,000 men would act boldly, in the hope that 100,000 others manning the defense lines of South Korea would not die," he later wrote. "I alone was responsible for tomorrow, and if I failed, the dreadful results would rest on judgment day against my soul."

For MacArthur, it was a portentous moment in an extraordinary life. The five-star general (one of only five Army officers who attained the rank) was standing at the pinnacle of a career that had stretched more than half a century. At age 70, MacArthur was the Supreme Commander for the Allied Powers, a position that made him the de facto leader of Occupied Japan and its 82 million citizens. Simultaneously, he was the

Commander in Chief of the United Nations Command, a position that made him the military leader of the allied forces in the Korean War, which to this point had been a bitterly fought defensive action.

With Chromite, MacArthur hoped to quickly transform the war through a decisive victory, and as anyone who lived through or studied the Korean conflict well knows, it was a resounding success. The invasion of Inchon reaffirmed MacArthur's reputation as a brilliant strategist. The plan, on which he had been forced to wager his power and reputation to obtain approval, was flawlessly executed. With the precision of a diamond cutter, MacArthur applied military pressure at the single most unlikely point and created a shining victory that turned the course of the Korean War.

With the success of Chromite, the General's career reached a new zenith. For those few weeks in the autumn of 1950, the entire world seemed to be ringing with praise for Douglas MacArthur. Although it would not last, there were few for the moment who would have contested Winston Churchill's assessment: "In trading space for time and in the counter-attack MacArthur did a perfect job."

With benefit of hindsight, we can see that Chromite's overwhelming victory also contained the seeds of MacArthur's downfall. It compelled the Communist Chinese to enter the war en force. Further, the power and influence that MacArthur gained in its aftermath acted as an accelerant in his ongoing conflict with President Harry Truman. In April 1951, this conflict would result in MacArthur's ignominious recall and a national controversy.

The Lessons of Inchon

The story of Operation Chromite is a good place to briefly introduce a few of the many lessons that MacArthur offers contemporary students of leadership. By 1950, MacArthur had had a half-century-long military career that was astonishingly rich in both achievement and diversity of experience. He brought the accumulated weight and integrated application of his experience, learning, and intuition to the conception, planning, and execution of the invasion at Inchon.

Chromite itself dated to the earliest days of the war. Prior to the outbreak of the Korean War, there had been skirmishes on and around the 38th Parallel, the artificial borderline between North and South Korea imposed by the Allies in 1945. But South Korea was deemed to have a strong military, and some observers even believed that its outspoken nationalist government was more likely to invade North Korea than vice versa. Thus, on June 24, 1950, when the North Korean People's Army (NKPA) swarmed across the 38th Parallel, South Korea and its allies were taken by surprise. By June 28, the South Korean capital of Seoul had fallen, and the defending army was in a state of collapse. On the next day, MacArthur, who was then leading the postwar occupation and revitalization of Japan, flew to Korea to see the situation first hand.

The general and his party landed 20 miles south of Seoul at an airport that had been bombed by the North Koreans just hours before. He traveled by car to the Han River on Seoul's south side, to a point where enemy mortar shells were exploding approximately 100 yards away. Here, he stopped to examine the fighting and the deportment of the troops. This personal reconnaissance on a battle's front line was a MacArthur trademark. "I cannot fight them if I cannot see them," he first declared in World War I.

During his one-day visit, MacArthur's observations of the South Korean troops led him to the immediate conclusion that the army of the Republic of Korea (ROK) was defeated and that the introduction of U.S. ground forces would be necessary to stop the North Koreans from completely overrunning South Korea. Standing on the Han, facing the loss of the entire Korean Peninsula, MacArthur then did something else that was entirely in character. He began planning his campaign strategy.

This almost immediate leap from observation to strategic planning was also a MacArthur trademark. Before President Truman committed ground troops to Korea and before he had formally assigned MacArthur command of the U.S. forces in Korea, MacArthur was already thinking through the defensive strategy and logistics that would be required to maintain a foothold in South Korea. Further, and in yet another MacArthur trademark, the General's mind just as quickly moved from defense to offense.

Later, MacArthur described his thought process while standing on the bank of the Han River. He said, "[I]n these reflections the genesis of the

Inchon operation began to take shape—a counter-stroke that could in itself wrest victory from defeat." Thus, the conception of the Inchon invasion was firmly rooted in the famous precept that guided MacArthur's approach to command: "In war, there is no substitute for victory."

Just three days later, the General launched the planning effort for Operation Bluehearts, the first iteration of his counteroffensive. The importance that MacArthur placed on speed of movement was obvious in Bluehearts; the invasion was initially scheduled to begin on July 22, less than a month after the start of the war. "The history of failure in war can almost be summed up in two words: Too Late," he wrote.

In fact, in early July, the larger logistical challenge of mobilizing for the Korean War and the need to reinforce the existing defense of South Korea in order to maintain a foothold on the Peninsula forced a frustrated MacArthur to postpone Bluehearts. But, in the two months of bitter fighting that followed, he led an aggressive and costly defense designed to first, delay and then, stalemate the North Koreans. Throughout that critical period and in keeping with his primary precept, MacArthur was also actively planning the assault that would enable a two-pronged counteroffensive aimed at enveloping and destroying the enemy army. He told the Joint Chiefs of Staff:

> *Every human effort in this command is now geared to the overriding first essential—to halt the enemy advance. [The enemy] is utilizing all major avenues of approach and has shown himself both skillful and resourceful in forcing or enveloping such roadblocks as he has encountered. Once he is fixed, it will be my purpose fully to exploit our air and sea control and, by amphibious maneuver, strike behind his mass of ground force.*

Toward that end, Macarthur renamed the invasion plan Operation Chromite and set a new date for mid-September. To many of MacArthur's peers and superiors, Chromite's target, the port city of Inchon, hardly seemed an auspicious choice. Inchon's 30-foot tides, second only to the Bay of Fundy, are so extreme that it would be accessible to the invasion's landing craft on only two days in September 1950. The daily fluctuations further limited access to three-hour windows. Any delay and/or unexpected resistance from the North Koreans could easily strand the invaders. Also, Inchon was many miles behind the front lines. If the North Koreans could stop the existing UN forces from breaking out at Pusan, they could isolate and overwhelm the invasion force.

These difficulties were exactly why MacArthur was so adamant in his choice of Inchon. "In war, surprise is decisive," said the General. He was convinced that the North Koreans would never expect or prepare for such an attack, so it would succeed.

In a series of meetings, conferences, and communiqués, MacArthur used all of his much-vaunted communication skills to gain approval for Chromite. The crucial meeting came on August 23, when according to MacArthur, the Army Chief of Staff and Chief of Naval Operations flew from Washington to Tokyo to "not so much discuss as to dissuade" him from attempting the landing at Inchon.

First, MacArthur listened to the numerous arguments against Inchon and to presentations of alternative plans for an invasion at Kunsan, a port further to the south and closer to the UN Forces at Pusan. He then launched, without notes, into what was by all accounts a convincing and compelling argument that stretched on for 45 minutes.

An avid student of the lessons of military history, MacArthur compared Chromite to British General James Wolfe's capture of Quebec in the French and Indian War almost 200 years before. Wolfe's equally unexpected plan called for 5,000 men to scale sheer 170-foot cliffs, on which the French had only light defenses, to gain position behind the fortified French city. The French lost the battle that followed on the Plains of Abraham, the city, and eventually, Canada itself. "Like Wolfe, I could take them by surprise," MacArthur declared.

Next, the General refuted the objections to Inchon. He said that the Navy was underestimating its own capabilities; he had "more confidence in the Navy than the Navy had in itself." He also eliminated the Kunsan option as one that would only extend the existing front and not trap the NKPA.

MacArthur reiterated Inchon's position as the proper place to cut the NKPA's supply lines. In the strongest terms, he declared the urgency of the situation and urged his superiors to act decisively:

> *Make the wrong decision here—the fatal decision of inertia—and we will be done. I can almost hear the ticking of the second hand of destiny. We must act now or we will die.*

MacArthur concluded his argument with a direct statement of responsibility and accountability. He promised to personally oversee the invasion and withdraw quickly if the plan went awry. "The only loss then will be to my professional reputation," he said. "But Inchon will not fail. Inchon will succeed." On September 8, the Joint Chiefs of Staff approved Operation Chromite.

MacArthur's confidence was a leadership trait that was evident throughout his career, but it was rarely sheer bravado. His choice of targets and operational plans were always informed by military intelligence and reconnaissance. "Battles are not won by arms alone," he said.

Prior to Inchon, information collected from prisoner-of-war interrogations suggested that the NKPA had approximately 1,000 poorly trained troops in that area and confirmed that no attack was expected. MacArthur also had the benefit of direct reconnaissance derived from covert missions. Two weeks before the invasion, Eugene Clark, a Navy lieutenant attached to MacArthur's G-2 (Intelligence) staff, was dispatched to Inchon, where he reported on the islands and conditions in the channel and harbor. Clark's information on tides, enemy strengths, mines, and other defenses confirmed Inchon's vulnerability. It was also used to target and destroy enemy fortifications prior to the landing. While MacArthur was waiting aboard the *Mount McKinley*, Clark was turning on the lamp at the Palmido lighthouse that would guide Task Force 90 up Flying Fish Channel to Inchon.

The fact that MacArthur was actually aboard the flagship was also in keeping with the General's approach to leadership. Throughout his life and after, MacArthur has been criticized for being both too close to the front lines of battle on some occasions *and* too far away on others. In reality, he tended to want to be close to the front.

MacArthur believed in *visible* leadership as a motivational force. Perhaps more importantly, he wanted to be close enough to personally observe the battle in high-risk operations such as Inchon and to be able to quickly adjust his plans when necessary. MacArthur often labeled such an operation a "reconnaissance in force," and he ensured adaptability and speed in decision-making by being present on the scene. Thus, on the day of the invasion, MacArthur commandeered a barge for an even closer look at the action. On September 17, he went ashore and drove east through Inchon into the combat zone itself.

As it turned out, there was no need to adjust Chromite. By the end of the invasion's first day, the U.S. Marines had captured a secure foothold at Inchon—roughly 150 miles behind the bulk of the NKPA and the hotly contested front lines of the Korean War.

The Inchon invasion was a catastrophic surprise to the North Koreans. As U.S. troops and supplies streamed ashore, the NKPA's supply lines were cut from behind, and the enemy army found itself trapped. When the North Koreans turned to face the threat to their rear, the pressure eased on the combined ROK, U.S., and UN forces, which had been bottled up behind the Pusan Perimeter, their final 100-mile-by-50-mile foothold in the southeastern corner of the Korean Peninsula. South Korea's defenders launched a full-fledged offensive and broke out.

Caught between two pincers, just as MacArthur had planned, the North Korean army was soon decimated. In the month of September, the UN Command recorded 130,000 enemy captured and 200,000 enemy casualties. It was estimated that only 25,000 NKPA troops made it back above the 38th Parallel.

The initial goal of the war, the liberation of South Korea, was accomplished in short order. On September 29, MacArthur formally restored Seoul to the Republic of Korea President Syngman Rhee. By the final week of October, the UN forces, under the command of MacArthur, had driven north of the 38th Parallel. In fact, they occupied the North Korean capital of Pyongyang and had reached as far as Chosan, a city hard on the Yalu River—the border between North Korea and Communist China.

A Leader Worth Knowing

As dramatic and successful as Operation Chromite was, it remains just one event in a life that offers a wealth of lessons to contemporary and future leaders. Throughout his adult life, Douglas MacArthur (as you will see in greater detail in Chapter 2) held an impressive array of top leadership positions in a variety of disciplines—including the military, public administration, education, sports, and business.

MacArthur's most dramatic leadership roles were those related to command positions in wartime. He personally led troops in World War I as the Rainbow Division's chief of staff and briefly was its leader and the youngest divisional commander of the war. In World War II, MacArthur first served as the Commanding General of the U.S. Army Forces in the Far East. He was then appointed Commander in Chief of the Southwest Pacific area and finally Commander in Chief of the U.S. Army Forces in the Pacific. In the Korean War, as we have seen, he served as the Commander in Chief of the United Nations Command.

Although MacArthur's military accomplishments garnered comparisons with Robert E. Lee and earned him a leading position among the nation's greatest commanders, his work as an organizational leader and public administrator was equally impressive. MacArthur served as the Army's Chief of Staff through the Great Depression. He was a Field Marshal in the Philippines and responsible for the development of that nation's military forces. Most notably, he oversaw the occupation and recovery of postwar Japan as Supreme Commander for the Allied Powers.

In education, MacArthur served as Superintendent of West Point. In sports, he was appointed President of the American Olympic Committee and led the U.S. team in the 1928 Olympics in Amsterdam. Entering the world of business after his "retirement," MacArthur accepted a position as Chairman of the Board of Remington Rand Corporation, which after several mergers, is now known as Unisys Corporation.

MacArthur's accomplishments as a leader in a variety of positions and disciplines suggest that his principles and approach can be effective in a wide range of organizations. The longevity of his career, the diversity of its circumstances, and the magnitude of the changes his world underwent (as a child, MacArthur lived on a frontier army post during the final years of the Indian Wars; in his final years, astronauts were routinely orbiting the earth) suggest that lessons derived from his experiences can be relevant to today's leaders.

This book contains 50 of General MacArthur's lessons for leaders. They are drawn from the General's life and career, and they are described and illustrated by his own words whenever possible. MacArthur's lessons are organized into four categories, each of which is presented in a dedicated section, as follows.

Principles of Strategy

Part Two presents 14 principles representing an inside look at the thinking and process of MacArthur, the master strategist. First and foremost, great leaders in every field of endeavor are visionaries and strategists. They must be able to choose the goals they and their organizations will pursue and then, design strategies capable of attaining them. MacArthur was an expert at both tasks.

MacArthur's ability to envision and prioritize goals was much in evidence in his peacetime activities. For instance, he pursued a new educational curriculum during his stewardship of West Point, one that would prepare cadets for the modern version of warfare that had emerged in World War I. Typically, in wartime, MacArthur's ultimate goals, such as defeating the Japanese or restoring South Korea to its citizens, were established by the U.S. government. But even when goals were imposed on him, MacArthur usually quickly adopted them as his own and pursued them with all of his energy.

Strategy was MacArthur's forte and, based on operations such Chromite, he earned a well-deserved reputation as a brilliant military strategist. Although no strategist is infallible, during WWII and in the opening months of the Korean War, creative leaps in strategic thinking seemed to become an almost effortless and natural activity for MacArthur. Witness how the initial plan for Chromite emerged during the General's first visit to the front lines of the Korean War. But like any highly experienced and well-practiced professional, MacArthur's talent for strategy was learned and honed over the years, and it was based on observation, sound thinking, and practical conclusions.

Inspirational Leadership

Part Three presents eight lessons that describe MacArthur's approach to motivational leadership. A leader must, by definition, have followers. To effectively execute strategies and successfully achieve goals, great leaders must motivate those followers to act. Throughout his career, MacArthur exhibited an extraordinary ability to inspire his followers to act.

MacArthur combined command authority, charismatic image, and a paternal humanity into a leadership persona that sustained him throughout his career. Using this model, he could influence and motivate a wide variety of people. On his command, tens of thousands of soldiers risked their lives, and 80 million citizens of Japan embraced radical cultural change and a new constitution and government.

MacArthur adjusted the scale of his leadership persona to the circumstances in which he found himself. Thus, he could effectively lead a small group as well as a nation using the same basic approach. Whether his followers were soldiers or citizens, they responded to his confidence-inspiring bearing and manner. They recognized his intellect and his dramatic flair. Although MacArthur was neither seen as a "common man" nor beloved as a "man of the people," he was nevertheless widely respected by those who did not have direct contact with him. More tellingly, among his direct subordinates, MacArthur was almost universally admired, and many of them remained loyal to him throughout their lives.

Organizational Management

Part Four presents 12 lessons that draw on MacArthur's experiences in organizational management. Today, it is widely recognized that the structure and management of organizations has a significant impact on strategic execution and goal achievement. MacArthur was an expert administrator and people manager.

The drama of MacArthur's life and career can obscure his competence as an executive. His approach to the occupation of Japan still stands as one of the few successful occupations in history and offers significant lessons for those public administrators who are struggling to establish and encourage new governments in Iraq and Afghanistan. Over half a century ago, MacArthur was building the kind of sleek, fast-response organizations that many business leaders are pursuing today. Today's merger and acquisition experts can learn much from his ability to create efficient, integrated structures out of collections of preexisting organizations.

By most measures, MacArthur was a superb manager of people. He was an excellent boss who understood the fine balance between personal control and delegation. He knew how to coax the highest level of performance from his subordinates. The conflict with Truman notwithstanding, he was also skilled at managing up. MacArthur had an enviable ability to persuade his superiors—from U.S. presidents to the Congress to the Joint Chiefs of Staff—to adopt policies and approve strategic and budgetary plans with which they initially disagreed.

Life and Career Management

Part Five presents a final set of 16 lessons that delve into the personal beliefs, traits, and skills that supported MacArthur's achievements as a leader. Great leaders develop and manage themselves before and after they take on the work of leading others. MacArthur embraced his future as a leader at an early age, and he managed his own life and career to maximize that future.

MacArthur was an early adherent of value-based leadership. Values, particularly West Point's "Duty, Honor, Country" played a large role in his success. MacArthur's values served as the foundation on which he based his life, the guideposts by which he navigated his career, and the basic criteria by which he judged himself and others.

As for personal traits and skills, MacArthur was fortunate to be born with some inherent advantages—such as family connections, intelligence, and a phenomenal memory—which aided him in his life and career. But in and of themselves, these traits were not enough to take him to the heights that he achieved. MacArthur bolstered his natural advantages by learning and developing traits that were not birthrights.

Always in pursuit of excellence, MacArthur preached and practiced preparedness, confidence, and initiative. He trained himself to become a dedicated learner and remained a learner throughout his life, utilizing his extensive reading and knowledge of history to support the achievement of his goals. MacArthur was also a master of the art of communication. He was practiced in image-building and media presentation. Although he was criticized for self-aggrandizement, he was undeniably successful at manipulating the media in pursuit of worthy objectives.

A Results-Based Perspective

Virtually every reader who opens this book will have a preconceived opinion about Douglas MacArthur. He has been the subject of hundreds of books and films. *American Caesar*, the MacArthur biography by William Manchester, was a national bestseller; Gregory Peck played the title role in the feature film *MacArthur*.

Throughout his lifetime (and in the four decades since his death in 1964), MacArthur has been both widely admired and disparaged. His reputation has risen and fallen more than once. It, and the many events and controversies with which he was associated, will surely continue to be hotly argued in the future.

Today, like other great leaders of his generation, including Franklin Delano Roosevelt and Winston Churchill (both distant relatives of his, by the way), MacArthur is often the subject of revisionist criticism. Sometimes the criticism is justified, but we have found that it often exaggerates a flaw or foible and underplays MacArthur's actual achievements. Perhaps this is a natural response to the iconic stature MacArthur attained and attempted to maintain during his lifetime. Perhaps it is simply because icons are really only caricatures of whatever they represent and are thus easy targets.

In any case, famous personages are judged in many ways. MacArthur has often been judged by his personality, beliefs, and image. He is also often judged with the benefit of 20/20 hindsight. Of course, he was not infallible and sometimes behaved in ways that were less than attractive (like most of us). But it is not our purpose to judge MacArthur from any of these perspectives.

We are interested in MacArthur as a leader; in that light, we have chosen to examine him based on his effectiveness as a leader and the results he obtained. Toward that end and before we detail the leadership lessons he offers, the next chapter of biography is meant to familiarize you, the reader, with his life and give you a chance to decide for yourself whether MacArthur was a leader worth knowing.

Chapter 2

A Leader's Destiny Fulfilled

Destiny is a word that both critics and admirers associate with Douglas MacArthur. His Virginia-born mother implanted a sense of destiny in her son at an early age, often telling him that he would become a great man, as great a soldier as his much-accomplished father and Robert E. Lee himself. From an early age, MacArthur appeared to wholeheartedly accept this destiny. He alluded to the role that destiny was playing in his life on many occasions, but he also worked hard to prepare for it and achieve it.

Reveille

"My first recollection is that of a bugle call," MacArthur was fond of saying. Indeed, on January 26, 1880, he was born to the khaki in the Arsenal Barracks in Little Rock, Arkansas, where his father, Arthur MacArthur, Jr., was posted with the 13th Infantry.

Arthur MacArthur was a significant military figure in his own right and obviously was a major influence on his son. In 1862, during the second year of the Civil War, he joined the Union Army as a first lieutenant. A courageous and aggressive fighter, he was cited for bravery and awarded a captaincy in his first battle at Perryville, Kentucky. Arthur was still a teenager when in November 1863, at the battle of Missionary Ridge in

Tennessee, he led the 24th Wisconsin Volunteers in an impromptu uphill charge under heavy fire and successfully captured the ridge. (After collecting collaborating statements and nominating himself, in 1889 he received the Medal of Honor for his actions.)

At 19 years of age, Arthur became the youngest colonel in the Union Army. After the war's conclusion in 1865, he made the Army his career, reenlisting as a second lieutenant. A decade later in 1875, Captain MacArthur married Mary "Pinky" Hardy of Norfolk, VA. Five years later, their third son, Douglas, was born.

Douglas MacArthur spent the first years of his life in Fort Wingate in the New Mexico Territory. His brother Malcolm, the family's second son, died of measles during this period. In 1884, a month after the ever-rebellious Geronimo and his Chiricahua Apaches surrendered once again, Arthur's company was reassigned, and four-year-old Douglas made the 300-mile march with his family to Fort Selden, overlooking the Rio Grande in the southeastern corner of the territory.

The next two years were an exciting time for the boy. "It was here I learned to ride and shoot even before I could read and write—indeed, almost before I could walk and talk," he remembered eight decades later. MacArthur's first schooling also began at Fort Selden. His parents tutored him, and the boy began to learn and adopt basic values. He wrote:

> *Our teaching included not only the simple rudiments, but above all else, a sense of obligation. We were to do what was right no matter what the personal sacrifice might be. Our country was always to come first. Two things we must never do: never lie, never tattle.*

After Selden, the MacArthur family moved to Fort Leavenworth, where the boy enjoyed watching the troops perform drills and artillery practice. Douglas did poorly, however, in his first three years of formal schooling. In 1889, the family moved once more, this time to Washington D.C., where his father was assigned a job in War Department.

In Washington, nine-year-old Douglas remained a lackadaisical student with average grades. He was, however, introduced to a more urbane way of life and came under the influence of his paternal grandfather. A retired associate justice of the Supreme Court of the District of Columbia, the first Arthur MacArthur was an active philanthropist and the author of numerous nonfiction books.

In 1892, Douglas's older brother, Arthur III, entered the U.S. Naval Academy at Annapolis and began a distinguished career of his own. (His life was unfortunately cut short when he died of appendicitis in 1923.) Douglas accompanied his parents to a new post at Fort Sam Houston in Texas in 1893.

Happy to return to the West, the 13-year-old was enrolled in the equivalent of ninth grade at the West Texas Military Academy in San Antonio. He suddenly blossomed as a student. He had somehow acquired the love of learning that would be evident throughout the rest of his life. "This is where I started," he said long after.

MacArthur's newfound interest in his studies resulted in superlative grades and a top rank in his class. The teenager also embraced athletics, a love he would maintain throughout his life. He became the school's best tennis player. In his senior year, he was quarterback of the football team, and manager and shortstop of the baseball team. Both teams recorded unbeaten seasons. In 1897, he graduated at the top of his class with a cumulative average of 96.67.

"Always before me was the goal of West Point," wrote MacArthur, "the greatest military academy in the world." But academic merit and the connections of his grandfather and father together were not enough to win him one of President Grover Cleveland's four appointments to the Academy. In hot pursuit of an appointment, the MacArthur family decided to split up. When Douglas's father was transferred to St. Paul, MN, he and his mother moved to Milwaukee, WI, where Congressman Theabold Otjen had announced a competitive examination for an appointment to West Point.

MacArthur spent the next 18 months preparing for the exam. He reentered high school and engaged two tutors. When President McKinley was elected, MacArthur tried and failed once more to gain a presidential appointment. In May 1898, on the morning of Otjen's test, Pinky told the nauseated boy, "Doug, you'll win if you don't lose your nerve." And he did. In June, it was announced that MacArthur had scored a 93.3, more than 13 points higher than the next-highest grade.

That summer, Arthur MacArthur, now a brigadier general of volunteers, was sent to the Philippines for the short-lived Spanish-American War. Peace negotiations were already in process in August 1898 when, after a brief fight, Manila was captured, and Arthur was named the city's military governor. In 1899, after the United States purchased the Philippines from Spain, he played a leading role in the ensuing war with Filipino insurgents led by Emilio Aguinaldo.

In a foreshadowing of events in his son's career, Arthur MacArthur was eventually appointed military governor of the islands, and he created plans for the establishment of a new government. He also ran afoul of politics when the responsibility for governing was split with a U.S. civil commission led by William Howard Taft. Their disagreements and Taft's complaints to Washington would harm his career in coming years. In July 1901, Taft took over as civil governor, and Arthur MacArthur (now a major general) returned to the United States.

The Young Soldier

While his father was in the Philippines, Douglas and his mother moved to West Point. In June 1899, Pinky took up residence in a nearby hotel; she would see her son virtually every day. Nineteen-year-old MacArthur plunged wholeheartedly into the life of a cadet.

MacArthur's performance at West Point was superlative in every aspect. He ranked first in his class in three of four years, finishing with a 98.14 average—the highest in twenty-five years. He had perfect scores in English, history, and law. Ironically, because he chose to join the Corps of Engineers upon graduation (it offered the fastest advancement track), his lowest grades were in engineering and drafting.

MacArthur himself suggested that his academic achievements were attributable to "perhaps, a somewhat clearer perspective of events—a better realization that first things come first." The ability to prioritize was always an obvious MacArthur skill and, by all reports, long hours of study were one of his priorities at West Point. What appears to have been a photographic memory must have also played a significant role. For instance, when MacArthur was not able to understand a complex text on "the space-time theory later formulated by Einstein as his Theory of Relativity," he simply memorized it.

MacArthur's leadership abilities became obvious at the Academy. He was a corporal in his second year and a sergeant in his third. MacArthur became first captain (the school's highest-ranking cadet) in his last year. In later years, fellow cadets would remember his soft-spoken and low-key authoritativeness.

After graduation in June 1903, MacArthur was commissioned as a second lieutenant in the Corps of Engineers and was sent to the Philippines for his first assignment. He supervised minor construction projects and surveyed various military locations, earning excellent ratings from his superiors. He was promoted to first lieutenant ten months after his arrival.

When a pair of bandits ambushed him while on a work detail in the jungle, MacArthur proved his presence of mind under fire. "Like all frontiersman, I was expert with a pistol," he said. "I dropped them both dead in their tracks, but not before one blazed away at me with his antiquated rifle." The bullet passed through his hat. It was the first of many brushes with death and perhaps the genesis of MacArthur's oft-stated conviction that he would not be killed in combat.

Malaria, not bandits, ended MacArthur's stay in the Philippines. In October 1904, he returned to the United States and various engineering assignments in California during his recovery. A year later, he was reassigned as an aide-de-camp to his father.

MacArthur traveled to Japan where he joined his father, now a military attaché, and his mother. A few days later, the family embarked on a military tour of the Far East. The 19,000-mile tour, which took the better part of a year, included stops in Japan, China, Malaysia, the Dutch East Indies, Burma, India, Ceylon, Siam, and Vietnam. MacArthur called it "the most important factor of preparation in my entire life." He returned to the United States in August 1906, convinced that "the future and, indeed, the very existence of America, were irrevocably entwined with Asia and its island outposts." It would also be true for his future.

The grand tour marked the beginning of the end of Arthur MacArthur's career. Taft was now Secretary of War, and although Arthur was a lieutenant general and ranking officer, he was passed over for the position of Chief of Staff. He headed the Pacific Division for less than a year and then was ordered to Milwaukee to write a report about his Far Eastern tour. He remained there without any significant assignment until his retirement in June 1909, a few months after Taft assumed the presidency.

Douglas MacArthur received a promising assignment to the Engineer School of Application in Washington D.C. He also served as a social aide-de-camp to President Theodore Roosevelt. However, in August 1907 he began an undistinguished assignment to the district office of engineers in Milwaukee, where his parents were residing.

MacArthur was next transferred to Fort Leavenworth, KS, where he was given his first company command. While there, he received a less-than-stellar efficiency report from his previous assignment. MacArthur vigorously but unsuccessfully contested the report. Then, he demonstrated his resiliency and determination to excel by pouring his energy into his current assignment.

MacArthur transformed K Company from the lowest-ranked of 21 companies into "champions" and said, "I could not have been happier if they had made me a general." He received an assignment as instructor of a new demolition course at nearby Fort Riley and wrote a manual to supplement it. At Leavenworth, he was appointed battalion adjutant and at various times served as quartermaster, commissary, and disbursing officer. In 1911, MacArthur's hard work paid off when he was promoted to captain and appointed head of the Department of Engineering.

A Rising Star

On September 5, 1912, Arthur MacArthur died suddenly during a reunion of his Civil War comrades. Of his father's death, Douglas said, "Never have I been able to heal the wound in my heart."

MacArthur requested a new assignment in Milwaukee to be near his mother, who was in poor health. Instead, a new world of opportunity opened when Leonard Wood, who had served under Arthur MacArthur in New Mexico and was now the Army's Chief of Staff, decided to intercede and offered MacArthur a position on his personal staff. The now-32-year-old captain quickly accepted and moved with Pinky to Washington.

MacArthur was first assigned to study disputed lands in the Canal Zone and quickly impressed Wood with his analysis and work ethic. In April 1913, he served a short stint as Superintendent of the State, War, and Navy Building. And in September of that year, having proved to be able, MacArthur was appointed to the 38-member General Staff. "My selection as its junior member brought me into intimate contact with the senior officers of the Army and Navy," said MacArthur, "and afforded me the rare opportunity of participating in highest command without the burden of final responsibility."

When war with Mexico loomed in 1914, Wood dispatched MacArthur to the U.S.-occupied port of Veracruz. MacArthur quickly decided that the lack of railroad engines of the proper gauge would delay any large expedition into the interior and conceived a covert mission to locate the necessary engines in Mexican-controlled territory. Six days after his arrival, at dusk on May 6, MacArthur left the safety of the occupied area. With three Mexican nationals, he located the engines, came under fire and narrowly escaped capture several times, and returned safely to Veracruz the next morning. The adventure earned him a nomination for the Medal of Honor; when the review board denied him the award, MacArthur contested the decision—to no avail.

That same year, World War I broke out in Europe, and military preparedness took on a new urgency. Promoted to major in December 1915, MacArthur assisted in the drafting of the National Defense Act of June 1916, a comprehensive package of laws designed to substantially strengthen the military and mobilize the economy in case of war. Also in June, MacArthur became the Army's first media-relations officer when he was assigned a newly created post as military assistant in charge of the War Department's Bureau of Information.

After President Wilson declared war against Germany in April 1917, MacArthur was instrumental in the presidential order to call up the National Guard. He also participated in the creation of the 42nd (or Rainbow) Division, which was comprised of Guard units drawn from states across the nation. On August 4, MacArthur was promoted to colonel and named the Rainbow's chief of staff.

The Fighting Dude

On November 1, 1917, MacArthur and the Rainbow arrived in France. Major General John J. Pershing's staff, which managed the American Expeditionary Force (AEF), decided to break up the new division for use as replacements. MacArthur and Rainbow commander General Mann responded with an energetic campaign to save the division. They bypassed normal channels by taking their case directly to Pershing's chief of staff and sent cables to powerful friends to Washington. In what would become an oft-used tactic, MacArthur used the press to try to enlist the support of the American media and public. (The stories were censored.) The campaign quickly established MacArthur as something of a maverick, but it was successful.

In light of MacArthur's performance in France in 1918 and 1919, the defamatory "Dugout Doug" appellation that emerged in the early years of World War II becomes even more ludicrous. He was one of the rare staff officers who insisted on participating in attacks as well as planning them.

In February 1918, within days of reaching the front at Lunéville, MacArthur accompanied his first raiding party into enemy territory. He assisted in the capture of several German prisoners. On March 9, MacArthur accompanied another raid in Salient du Feys. His commanding officer wrote the following:

> *...in the face of the determined and violent resistance of an alert enemy, he lent actual advice on the spot to the unit commanders and by his supervision of the operations not only guaranteed its success, but left with the entire division the knowledge of the constant attention of their leaders to their problems in action, and a sense of security which his wise and courageous leadership there impressed on the engaged companies.*

MacArthur seemed intent on establishing a casual, yet immediately recognizable leadership image, one that communicated experience and authoritativeness. In spite of regulations, he refused to wear a gas mask. He did not carry a weapon or wear a helmet on raids. His dress also set him apart: He wore a turtleneck sweater and muffler, and removed the support from his hat (so it appeared well-worn and less rigid). He carried a riding crop. He quickly attracted nicknames such as "the Dude" and "D'Artagnan of the AEF."

At the end of March 1918, the Rainbow became the first American division to be given control of a full sector—the Baccarat area on the Lorraine front—and its leaders took an aggressive stance. Of its three months in the sector, MacArthur said, "For eighty-two days the division was in almost constant combat."

In late May, the Germans launched a major offensive and advanced to within 50 miles of Paris. The Rainbow, which had suffered 2,000 casualties since entering combat in February, was redeployed to help stop the German advance. MacArthur was promoted to brigadier general, the youngest at that time in the AEF. The announcement from the Secretary of War Newton Baker's office said that MacArthur "is by many of his seniors considered the most brilliant young officer in the army."

In mid-July, MacArthur and the 42nd defended against the main attacks in a pitched four-day battle that rebuffed Germany's Champagne-Marne offensive and effectively ended its chances of winning the war. In the midst of the celebration, however, the 38-year-old general seemed for the first time to wonder about the toll the war was taking:

> *A few nights later a group of us toasted our victory in Chalons. We drank to the petit barmaids and sang...but I found something missing. It may have been the vision of those writhing bodies hanging from the barbed wire or the stench of dead flesh still in my nostrils. Perhaps I was just getting old; somehow, I had forgotten how to play.*

The fighting, however, was far from over. As the Allies took the offensive, the Rainbow was reassigned to the Fere Forest near Chateau-Thierry and plunged back into battle during the Aisne-Marne offensive. At the end of July, MacArthur took over as acting commander of the 84th Brigade and led the fighting from the front lines.

In September 1918, the Rainbow and MacArthur fought in the first American-led offensive at St. Mihiel. Although a difficult battle was anticipated, the Germans abandoned their positions before it began. As the 84th drove forward, it captured approximately 500 enemy troops.

By mid-October, the Rainbow was fighting once again, this time in the Romagne Woods in the bitter Meuse-Argonne offensive. By early November, the Americans were threatening Sedan, and for 12 days, MacArthur became the youngest divisional commander of the war when he was given command of the Rainbow. On November 11, 1918, the armistice was signed, and World War I ended.

After a five-month stint in the Army of Occupation, the Rainbow Division was shipped home. For his heroism and leadership during the war, General MacArthur was awarded the Distinguished Service Cross twice, the Distinguished Service Medal, seven Silver Stars, and (years later) two Purple Hearts. The French awarded him the Croix de Guerre twice and made him a Commander in the Legion of Honor.

On April 25, 1919, the Rainbow disembarked in New York. But instead of cheering crowds, they found only "one little urchin" on the pier. In a letter to a former aide written a few weeks later, MacArthur wrote: "Amid a silence that hurt—with no one, not even the children to see us—we marched off the dock, to be scattered to the four winds—a sad, gloomy end of the Rainbow."

An Executive Emerges

A few days after his return, the Army chief of staff informed MacArthur that his next post would be Superintendent of West Point. At age 39, he was one of the youngest superintendents ever appointed and was responsible for the cornerstone of the Army's officer corps.

MacArthur's mandate, effective June 12, 1919, was to "revitalize and revamp the Academy." The art and science of warfare had been radically altered during WWI, but the staff at the academy had been steadfastly resisting changes in the curriculum. Further, the war's insatiable demand for officers resulted in lowered entrance standards and in the program being temporarily reduced to one year. Thus, the cadet corps' class system, which plays a major role in transmitting the traditions of the Army, had been decimated.

For the next three years, MacArthur worked to expand the curriculum and create a broader education in the liberal arts. The study of war was updated to include the lessons of WWI; the curriculum in the hard sciences was updated to reflect advances in electronics, internal combustion engines, and aerodynamics. MacArthur also changed the standards for instructors, requiring that they experience the methods used at other colleges and universities and improve their own teaching skills.

MacArthur replaced the annual summer camp (which was more vacation than education) with Regular Army training at Camp Dix in New Jersey. Concerned with the physical fitness of the cadets, he strongly supported athletics and introduced mandatory intramural sports. At the same time, MacArthur reinforced the traditional values of the academy. It was he who institutionalized the cadet's honor code. He set the cadets themselves to work on a plan to reduce and control hazing.

As a superintendent promoting change, MacArthur ruffled many feathers at the Academy, as well as in the office of Army Chief of Staff "Black Jack" Pershing. In early 1922, he was notified that he was being reassigned a year earlier than usual, and many of his changes at West Point were undone in the next several years. In decades after, however, almost all the changes were reinstituted, and today MacArthur is remembered as the architect of many of the features of the modern West Point.

After West Point, MacArthur was sent back to the Philippines. In October 1922, he arrived with his new wife, a rich divorcee named Louise Cromwell Brooks, and her two children. He first met Louise while at West Point, and on Valentine's Day 1922, at age 42, he married for the first time. (The MacArthurs separated in 1927 and were divorced in 1929.)

MacArthur was given light duty: the command of the newly created Military District of Manila. Subsequently, he commanded the Philippine Division's 23rd Brigade. He learned a great deal about the islands during this period and met many of the Philippine leaders with whom his future would be intertwined.

Just days after Pershing retired in September 1924, MacArthur's promotion to major general, the youngest on the active list, was announced. In the next few years, he successfully completed assignments in the United States as commander of the Fourth, Third, and Ninth Corps.

In September 1927, ten months before the Ninth Olympiad in Amsterdam, the president of the American Olympic Committee died suddenly. MacArthur, who was commanding the Third Corps and whose support of athletics was well-established, was elected to the position. He accompanied the U.S. team to the Games in 1928 and proved as effective a coach as he was a commander. He later said:

> *Athletes are among the most temperamental of all persons, but I stormed and pleaded and cajoled. I told them we represented the greatest nation in the world, that we had not come 3,000 miles just to lose gracefully, that we were there to win, and win decisively.*

The team did just that. The United States finished first in the games, with more than twice as many points as its nearest competitor. It set seventeen Olympic records and seven world records.

In 1928, MacArthur returned to Manila, where he commanded the Army forces in the islands as head of the Philippine Department. He remained there for two years; President Herbert Hoover then raised him to the top of the Army's leadership hierarchy. On November 21, 1930, at age 50, MacArthur was sworn in as the Army's Chief of Staff.

Over the next five years, the Great Depression swallowed up the economies of many of the world's major nations, and MacArthur was forced to fight a constant battle to maintain the size and preparedness of the Army. During his tenure, the Army's budget shrank from $347 million in 1931 to $284 million in 1935. Given the economic environment and the concurrent growth of pacifistic sentiment in the general public, these losses seemed more like victories.

MacArthur set his priorities carefully. He pulled out all the stops to protect the Army Officer Corps, which he saw as the "mainspring of the whole mechanism" of national defense. He called for new and innovative equipment. He later said:

> *...I almost licked the boots of certain gentleman to get funds for motorization and mechanization and air power. I humbled myself seeking allotments to replace leaking, slum-like barracks housing for our soldiers. I called for increased speed, increased fire power, fast machines, airplanes, tanks, guns, trucks, and ammunition.*

MacArthur's urgency was driven by the rise of fascism. In the early 1930s, Hitler rose to power as dictator of Germany. In that same period, the Japanese attacked Manchuria and Shanghai. But MacArthur's appeals were largely unsuccessful. Instead, critics began to paint him as being overly militaristic and a "warmonger."

MacArthur's role in the Bonus Army incident added to this unfortunate image. In the summer of 1932, more than 20,000 WWI veterans and their families marched on Washington to pressure Congress into the early payment of service bonuses. On July 28, after the marchers rioted and two Washington D.C. policemen were killed, Hoover ordered MacArthur to clear the Bonus Army from the city. MacArthur led the action himself, but the marchers resisted. In the resulting chaos, approximately 40 people were injured and a baby died from tear gas inhalation. MacArthur would get far more than his fair share of blame.

The Bonus Army debacle contributed to Hoover's defeat in 1932 and the election of Franklin Delano Roosevelt. Under FDR, MacArthur continued to struggle for funding. He also oversaw the speedy formation and successful operation of the New Deal's Civilian Conservation Corps. FDR obviously found MacArthur to be an effective leader; he retained him as chief of staff for one and one-half years beyond the usual four-year term.

A Fighter for the Philippines

At age 55, and with 36 years invested in his career, MacArthur was not ready to retire. Instead, in what would turn out to be a momentous decision, he remained on active duty and became military advisor to the newly established Philippines Commonwealth and President Manuel Quezon. In this unique position, he simultaneously served as a major general in the U.S. Army *and* a field marshal of the Philippines Army.

MacArthur's job was to design and build an independent Filipino army capable of protecting the islands. It was widely accepted that the Philippines were indefensible, but MacArthur was convinced that the prevailing opinion was wrong. He believed that with a small air force, a fleet of short-range torpedo boats, and a large army of trained citizen-soldiers such as Switzerland's, the islands could be protected. Characteristically, he threw himself into the job, creating and leading a ten-year development plan.

In the midst of this work, Pinky MacArthur, who accompanied her son to his new post, died at age 84. MacArthur was desolate at the loss. In April 1937, he married for the second time—to Jean Marie Faircloth, a native of Murfreesboro, TN, whom he had met on the sea journey to the Philippines. It was to be a long and devoted relationship, and their son, Arthur MacArthur IV, was born in February 1938. MacArthur became a doting father at age 58.

In December 1937, MacArthur retired from the U.S. Army. His efforts on behalf of the Philippines military had caused political repercussions at home, and the War Department attempted to give him a new assignment in the States. MacArthur refused; he had no desire to return home to a lesser assignment and rank and remained committed to the task of building the Philippines Army. For the next three years, however, Japanese aggression accelerated and his funding declined. Time ran out halfway through the job.

In July 1941, FDR recalled 61-year-old MacArthur to active duty as a lieutenant general and named him commander of U.S. Forces in the Far East. On December 7, the Japanese attacked Pearl Harbor and destroyed the Pacific fleet. That afternoon, a similar attack was launched on the Philippines. Half the U.S. airpower in the islands, a critical element in their defense, was destroyed.

On December 22, Japan's Fourteenth Army landed at Lingayen Gulf to the north of Manila. MacArthur was unsuccessful in his bid to stop the invaders on the beach. As the Japanese drove toward Manila, he was forced "to sideslip my troops westward by a series of rapid maneuvers and holding actions to the rocky [Bataan] peninsula and Corregidor forts before their path could be cut from the north." The complex withdrawal worked, and the American and Filipino troops reached Bataan and the tiny island of Corregidor—where they were able to deny the Japanese access to Manila Bay and maintain a secure base for future attack.

The campaign in defense of the Philippines was predicated on the eventual arrival of relief. However, FDR had already committed to support the war in Europe as a first priority, and there would be no reinforcements. "Unhappily," said MacArthur, "I was not informed of any of these vital conferences and believed that a brave effort at relief was in the making."

In February 1942, with food and supplies dwindling and no relief in sight, FDR ordered MacArthur to Australia to assume command of the Southwest Pacific theater. MacArthur resisted. "I and my family will share the fate of the garrison," he told Army chief of staff George Marshall. On March 11, however, MacArthur followed orders and left Corregidor on a torpedo boat with his wife, son, and a small group of officers. It was a harrowing and successful escape, which Winston Churchill said, "...saved for all his future glorious services, the great Commander who would otherwise have perished or passed the war as a Japanese captive."

Two months later, a beleaguered Bataan fell, and on May 6, 1942, Corregidor followed. By June, the remaining American forces in the Philippines were forced to surrender. They had held out for longer than any other Allied stronghold in the Pacific and slowed the Japanese momentum for six months. This was four months longer than the Japanese had anticipated and at a time when the enemy was at its peak strength. Abandoned and understandably disillusioned, four in ten of the defenders would die on the Bataan Death March and in prison camps. A distraught MacArthur, who had received the Medal of Honor for his part in the doomed defensive, offered tribute:

> *Corregidor needs no comment from me. It has sounded its own story at the mouth of its guns. It has scrolled its own epitaph on enemy tablets. But through the bloody haze of its last reverberating shot, I shall always seem to see a vision of grim, gaunt, ghastly men, still unafraid.*

MacArthur's Return

MacArthur's high-profile role in the Pacific made him a heroic icon in the eyes of the American public, and he quickly became one of the nation's most admired leaders. He used this platform to transform the Philippines into an emotion-laden symbol for victory in the Pacific. Shortly after his arrival in Australia on March 17, 1942, he told reporters:

> *The President of the United States ordered me to break through the Japanese lines and proceed from Corregidor to Australia for the purpose, as I understand it, of organizing the American offensive against Japan, a primary object of which is the relief of the Philippines. I came through and I shall return.*

The last phrase became one of the most famous of the war, and MacArthur plunged into making it a reality. Although he commanded an entire theater of operations, he had practically no resources. Nevertheless, instead of preparing for the expected Japanese invasion of Australia at the "Brisbane Line," MacArthur took the fight to the enemy. "I decided to abandon the plan completely, to move the thousand miles forward into eastern Papua, and to stop the Japanese on the rough mountains of the Owen Stanley Range of New Guinea—to make the fight for Australia beyond its own borders," he said.

In August 1942, after the Japanese attacked over the 13,000-foot peaks running through the center of the Papua, MacArthur committed troops to defend the last Allied stronghold before Australia. They stopped the enemy advance before Port Moresby and also foiled a second amphibious attack at Milne Bay. With the Allied foothold on Papua secured, MacArthur took the offensive. In October, with the help of airlifts, the Australians drove the Japanese back over the Owen Stanley Range. In November, with newly arrived American troops to bolster his forces, MacArthur launched attacks over the mountains on Japanese strongholds at Buna and Gona. After bitter, costly battles in malaria-infested jungles, the Japanese were pushed out of Papua and into New Guinea.

The long fight back to the Philippines began. Over the next two years, MacArthur created and executed a series of operations that demonstrated his strategic brilliance. Using a "triphibious" strategy, he combined air, sea, and land forces to advance hundreds of miles at a clip. He also adopted a "hit 'em where they ain't" strategy. Instead of fighting the enemy head-on and moving from stronghold to stronghold, he used the geography of the southwest Pacific to sever lines of supply and communication and isolate Japanese forces. This strategy worked so well that hundreds of thousands of Japanese troops were effectively neutralized, whereas casualty numbers in MacArthur's theater were notably low.

By the summer of 1944, MacArthur was ready to fulfill his promise to return to the Philippines. The island of Mindanao was the chosen reentry point, but when it was discovered that Leyte was vulnerable, the plan was quickly changed. "Leyte was to be the anvil against which I hoped to hammer the Japanese into submission in the central Philippines—the springboard from which I would proceed to the conquest of Luzon, for the final assault against Japan itself," said MacArthur.

On October 20, 1944, with the most powerful Navy armada yet assembled at his back, MacArthur waded in and proclaimed over the radio, "People of the Philippines: I have returned."

The landing was successful, but the Japanese quickly responded with all the force they could muster. At sea, the U.S. Navy fought and won a decisive victory in the Battle of Leyte Gulf. The Japanese lost half its fleet in the four-day battle. On land, it was December before the Allied victory was clear, but Leyte was won and then so was the island of Mindoro. The way to Luzon and Manila was now clear.

On January 9, 1945, the battle for Luzon began with a massive amphibious landing at Lingayen Gulf, the same point from which the

Japanese had launched their invasion just over three years before. Now a five-star General of the Army, MacArthur came ashore four hours after the landings began.

The campaign for Luzon would last until the end of the war, when General Yamashita and 65,000 Japanese troops finally laid down their weapons. Well over 200,000 Allied troops fought; 10,000 died. More than 200,000 Japanese soldiers were killed. In the process, the city of Manila was destroyed, and 100,000 Filipino civilians died there.

On July 16, 1945, when the first atomic bomb was detonated in Alamogordo, NM, MacArthur was busy planning Operation Olympic. This operation, which was to be the first step in the invasion of Japan, was set for November 1945. It was estimated that one million Allied troops would be needed. Instead, atomic bombs were dropped on the cities of Hiroshima and Nagasaki on August 6 and August 9, 1945, respectively.

On August 10, the Japanese began to negotiate their surrender. Five days later, President Truman announced the end of the war. He appointed MacArthur to be Supreme Commander for the Allied Powers (SCAP) in Japan, and instructed him to arrange for and accept the formal surrender. World War II was over.

Japan's Proconsul

The SCAP appointment order contained the following clause: "From the moment of surrender, the authority of the Emperor and Japanese Government to rule the state will be subject to you and you will take such steps as you deem proper to effectuate the surrender terms." Thus, MacArthur became the de facto leader of Japan and its 71 million citizens. (This number increased to 83 million by 1950.)

On August 30, 1945, MacArthur, who was now beyond the Army's statutory retirement age of 64, flew into the Atsugi airport on the plane he had named *Bataan*. Unarmed and accompanied by a small party, he entered a nation that had been a bitter enemy until just days before. The twenty-mile drive to Yokohama took two hours. The sides of the streets were lined with armed Japanese soldiers and behind them stood crowds of civilians. It was an audacious act that instantly established both

MacArthur's authority and his trust in the Japanese people. Churchill later said, "Of all the amazing acts of bravery of the war, I regard MacArthur's landing at Atsugi as the greatest of the lot."

On September 2, MacArthur presided over the surrender ceremony aboard the battleship *Missouri*. "We must go forward to preserve in peace what we have won in war," he said, reiterating messages of peace and cooperation. "A new era is upon us."

As he set up headquarters in Tokyo's Dai Ichi Building, one of the few major buildings left standing in the capitol, MacArthur quickly discovered that Japan's condition was critical. More than six million civilians had died in the war; more than 100,000 perished in the two atomic blasts. Fifteen million people were homeless. The major cities were destroyed. Manufacturing capacity was one-third of prewar levels, and there were severe shortages of all essential materials.

One of MacArthur's first acts in Japan was to forbid the commandeering of food by the occupiers. He appropriated 3.5 million tons of U.S. Army food and gave it to the Japanese. When the House Appropriations Committee in Washington asked him to justify the act, he replied, "Give me bread or give me bullets."

In an early statement, MacArthur told the Japanese, "SCAP is not concerned with how to keep Japan down, but how to get her on her feet again." Over the next six years, as he oversaw the restructuring and rebuilding of Japan, that mission guided him through one of history's most successful occupations.

MacArthur's mandate included fundamental political, economic, and social reforms. He succinctly stated the ambitious and wide-ranging occupation goals:

> *First destroy the military power. Punish war criminals. Build the structure of representative government. Modernize the constitution. Hold free elections. Enfranchise the women. Release the political prisoners. Liberate the farmers. Establish a free labor movement. Encourage a free economy. Abolish police oppression. Develop a free and responsible press. Liberalize education. Decentralize political power. Separate church from state.*

The first several years of the occupation were focused on reform. MacArthur disarmed Japan. In the first months after the surrender, 2.5 million tons of guns and ammunition, almost 200,000 cannons, 100,000 tons of chemical weapons, 8,000 combat planes, and 2,500 tanks were destroyed. The remnants of the Japanese Navy were scuttled, scrapped, or transferred to Allied nations. Almost 7 million Japanese troops were returned to civilian life.

The country's system of governance was radically altered. MacArthur brilliantly handled the incendiary issue of Japanese Emperor Hirohito. In June 1945, a Gallup poll revealed that 93 percent of Americans thought that Hirohito should be deposed after the war; more than 30 percent felt he should be executed for war crimes. Conversely, the Japanese revered the Emperor as a god. Without inflaming either nation, MacArthur retained Hirohito and used him to bolster SCAP's authority; at the same time, he transformed the Emperor's role into a largely ceremonial one.

SCAP was instrumental in the preparation of a new Japanese constitution, one that was established on the English pattern and that stands to this day. In Article 9, the Japanese forever renounced the threat or use of war and banned the creation of a national military. Women's suffrage (13 million women voted for the first time in 1946), voter reform, and a free press were established.

With the guidance and prompting of SCAP, the Japanese adopted educational reforms and sweeping land reforms, which redistributed five million acres and created an agricultural base of small independent farmers. The power of the zaibatsu, the handful of family-controlled conglomerates that monopolized Japan's economy, was reduced. Labor unions were encouraged. In two years, the number of union members in Japan grew from under 1,000 to more than 6 million.

In 1947, as the Cold War and Japan's reforms took root, the emphasis of the occupation shifted to economic recovery. Japan was now seen as a valued ally in the Far East. That year, MacArthur authorized the display of the Japanese flag, which was banned after the surrender. He also began to be a vocal advocate for an end to the occupation. On March 17, 1947, he held a press conference and called for a treaty returning Japan's independence. (The treaty was signed in San Francisco on September 8, 1951; MacArthur was not in attendance.)

In the late 1940s, in accordance with orders from Washington, MacArthur began to institute the so-called Dodge Line to stabilize the Japanese economy with balanced budgets and anti-inflationary tactics.

The new economic program is credited with saving Japan's banking industry, but the ultimate results of these efforts would never be known. Soon, Japan's industrial companies would be flooded with military purchase orders for Korea, and the nation's economy would be off on a long, prosperous run.

A Limited Warrior

When the North Korean army overran the 38th Parallel on June 25, 1950, MacArthur unexpectedly returned to war at age 70. Korea would be a war unlike any other MacArthur had fought, and it would contain both the high and low points of his military life.

The outbreak of the war, MacArthur's plan to fight an aggressive defense to slow and stop the enemy, and the counterattack that began at Inchon were described in Chapter 1. Looming in the background of these events was the growing tension between MacArthur and the Truman administration.

The State Department and President Truman were frustrated by MacArthur's high profile and his willingness to make independent pronouncements to both the leaders of other nations and the media. MacArthur, on the other hand, rightly perceived a leadership vacuum in the Far East and, as was his wont, took the initiative to try and fill it.

In early August 1950, MacArthur drew flak for visiting the Chinese Nationalists on Formosa and implying that the United States would support them militarily. A few weeks later, he enraged Truman with a wired message on Formosa for the Veterans of Foreign Wars, which was released to major media outlets and published in full in the *New York Times* and *U.S. News & World Report*. Truman ordered MacArthur to withdraw it, and MacArthur exacerbated the tense situation by protesting.

The Inchon invasion in September initiated the destruction of the North Korean army and temporarily saved MacArthur. On the heels of the victory, he was given approval to move above the 38th Parallel and unify Korea. Truman, recognizing the achievement and fully understanding the political ramifications of any conflict with MacArthur, decided to take a positive approach to their sour relationship.

On October 15, 1951, three weeks before the congressional elections, Truman flew to Wake Island to meet his general for the first time. MacArthur saw the now-famous meeting as politically motivated (and it likely was). They briefly discussed the war, and Truman asked MacArthur about the chances of Chinese or Soviet intervention in Korea. MacArthur replied, "Very little."

Before leaving Wake Island that same day, Truman awarded MacArthur his fifth Distinguished Service Medal. At the same time, more than 300,000 Chinese troops were in the process of slipping across the Yalu River border and gathering in North Korea. In late October, they struck hard and then disappeared, leading MacArthur to believe that it was only a small force.

MacArthur responded by ordering a bombing campaign that was designed to cut off Chinese access to North Korea at the Yalu. Fearing a larger war if bombs fell too close to China, Truman's staff and the Joint Chiefs of Staff canceled the campaign. MacArthur protested, and (somewhat surprisingly) Truman decided to back him. The raids successfully destroyed their targets, and a heartened MacArthur announced that he hoped "to get the boys home by Christmas."

Unfortunately, the bulk of the Chinese troops never left North Korea, and they launched a major offensive on November 25. As the UN forces fought and were forced to retreat, MacArthur cabled the Joint Chiefs, "We face an entirely new war." MacArthur also vented his frustration publicly, which rekindled Truman's anger. On December 5, the President tried to muzzle MacArthur with directives that required all government employees to clear statements on foreign policy before release.

By January, after weeks of fighting in the bitter Korean winter, the UN forces (under the immediate command of General Matthew Ridgway, who was newly appointed by MacArthur after the death of General Walton Walker) were back below the 38th Parallel, and Seoul had fallen once again. In mid-January, in the midst of discussions about evacuating the troops, Ridgway rallied his forces, attacked, and began to regain ground. (By April, he would push the Chinese back beyond the 38th Parallel and hold his gains.)

MacArthur was convinced that Washington did not have the "will to win" the war, and he made uncleared statements to that effect. At the end of March, when Truman quietly attempted to initiate peace talks,

MacArthur purposely killed the effort with a public announcement, proclaiming that the Chinese were as good as beaten. Truman privately decided that MacArthur had to be relieved.

The final act came quickly. In early April, Congressman Joe Martin released a letter from MacArthur that criticized Truman's support of NATO and the whole concept of limited war. "There is no substitute for victory," wrote MacArthur, in what would become a much-echoed theme. On April 11, 1951, Truman responded by announcing the 71-year-old general's recall.

The effort to inform MacArthur of the recall was badly botched. News of the dismissal leaked out, and a staff member in Tokyo heard it on the radio. He interrupted a small dinner party to tell Jean MacArthur, and she whispered the news to her husband. The general said, "Jeannie, we're going home at last" and returned to his meal. Later, MacArthur declared that "No office boy, no charwomen, no servant of any sort would have been dismissed with such callous disregard for ordinary decencies."

Taps

Before dawn on April 16, 1951, an estimated one million Japanese citizens lined the route to the airport to bid farewell to MacArthur and his family. It was a show of respect and admiration that would be repeated many times in the months ahead.

In Honolulu, 100,000 islanders turned out for the first welcome home. On April 17, 1951, MacArthur set foot on the U.S. mainland for the first time in 14 years. A half-million San Franciscans turned the short trip from the airport into a parade.

MacArthur proceeded to Washington, where he addressed a joint session of Congress on April 19. Millions of Americans watched MacArthur deliver his now-famous "Old Soldiers Never Die" speech on television. Congressman wept; the applause went on for many minutes. After the thirty-seven minute speech, a quarter-million people saw MacArthur off to New York City.

In New York, the Waldorf-Astoria Hotel offered MacArthur a penthouse suite at a highly reduced rate. (He and Jean would live there for the rest of their lives.) The New York Police Department estimated that a record crowd of 7.5 million people turned out for the tickertape parade in his honor on April 20.

On May 3, 1951, MacArthur was the first witness to testify before hearings of the Senate Armed Services and Foreign Relations committees. He was on the stand for three days, and he detailed the beliefs and strategies that had placed him at odds with his superiors.

MacArthur next embarked on a year-long national tour of speeches and appearances that positioned him as possible candidate for the Republican presidential nomination. He was considered as a potential candidate in the previous three presidential elections, but he never actively campaigned.

As in the past, MacArthur appeared to be willing to serve if called, but he did not campaign in the traditional sense. In fact, he asked his supporters to support Senator Robert Taft for the nomination. By July 1952, MacArthur was a dark horse at best. He gave the keynote address at the Republican National Convention in Chicago, but, for once, he failed to galvanize his audience. Dwight Eisenhower, who served as MacArthur's aide in the 1930s, won the nomination and the presidency.

In August 1952, MacArthur took a job in the private sector. He became the chairman of the board of Remington Rand, Inc., at which he played an active role as an advisor to management. He attended meetings as often as four times per week in the company's Connecticut headquarters and addressed shareholder meetings. He also gave speeches supporting free enterprise and industry and attacking big government and excessive taxation.

In 1955, when the company merged with the Sperry Corporation, MacArthur was elected Chairman of the new Sperry Rand Corporation. By 1960, it was a billion-dollar company. MacArthur held the position for the remainder of his life.

In 1961, the 81-year old General was invited to the Philippines. On the fifteenth anniversary of Philippines' independence, he gave the keynote address to more than one million Filipinos.

The next year, the U.S. Congress passed a joint resolution that recognized "his outstanding devotion to the American people" and "his brilliant leadership during and following World War II." It also struck a gold medal in his honor. Both John F. Kennedy and Lyndon Johnson solicited MacArthur's advice during their presidencies. He advised both to avoid any military involvement in Vietnam.

In February 1964, MacArthur's health, which for several years had been in decline, became critical. He entered Walter Reed Army Medical Center, where his gall bladder was removed. Two more operations followed. On April 5, 1964, at age 84, he died of coronary thrombosis.

President Johnson had the flag at the White House lowered to half-mast and ordered a state funeral for MacArthur. "One of America's greatest heroes is dead," said Johnson. "But in the hearts of his countrymen and in the pages of history, his courageous presence among us and his valiant deeds for us will never die."

☆☆☆☆☆

PART TWO

PRINCIPLES OF STRATEGY

Chapter 3

Define and Pursue Victory

Every organization strives for victory in one way or another. Victory can mean winning a war, capturing market share, or reaching a fund-raising goal. But no matter how victory is defined, every successful organization must attain it. Leaders are responsible for defining what victory means, focusing the intention of the organization on it, and shepherding their followers in the quest to attain it.

MacArthur defined victory in various ways during his career. As Superintendent of West Point, victory meant producing a steady stream of new officers who were adept at modern methods of warfare and management. As Army Chief of Staff, victory meant maintaining the preparedness of the Army and Army Air Corps. And, most famously, as a general at war, victory meant defeating aggression and forcing the enemy to surrender. But one precept always remained fixed in MacArthur's mind: The definition of victory is the first determinate of strategy.

It was the definition of victory in the Korean War and its ramifications on military strategy that served as the root cause behind President Truman's recall of MacArthur. The Truman administration's definition of victory in Korea was never fixed; it changed as the circumstances of the war changed. After the Red Chinese entered the war, the administration's definition of victory became that of defensive stalemate.

Given the human cost of war, the idea of utilizing it in a limited way made no sense to MacArthur. When he addressed Congress on April 19, 1951, he said:

> *[O]nce war is forced upon us, there is no other alternative than to apply every available means to bring it to a swift end. War's very object is victory—not prolonged indecision. In war, indeed, there is no substitute for victory.*
>
> *There are some who for varying reasons would appease Red China. They are blind to history's clear lesson. For history teaches with unmistakable emphasis that appeasement but begets new and bloodier war. It points to no single instance where this end has justified that means—where appeasement has led to more than a sham peace. Like blackmail, it lays the basis for new and successively greater demands, until, as in blackmail, violence becomes the only other alternative. Why, my soldiers asked of me, surrender military advantages to an enemy in the field? I could not answer.*

As commander-in-chief, Truman should have—and did—win the debate with MacArthur. MacArthur accepted that authority and never challenged Truman's right to relieve him. Two years later, at the cost of tens of thousands of additional American casualties, the war ended on the 38th Parallel, where it had begun. In the 50+ years since, Korea has remained divided. North Korea is ruled by a dictator, who now claims to have nuclear weapons and threatens to use them when he wishes to gain political and economic concessions. And the question still remains: Would MacArthur's definition of victory, which included the commitment of all the force at the nation's disposal, ultimately have been more or less costly than Truman's limited definition?

MacArthur's ability to focus the organizational intention on victory is notable. He rallied the Allied effort in the southwest Pacific during WWII. It is doubtful that the Philippines would have been liberated before the end of the war if MacArthur had not focused the attention of the world on that goal. Like Germany and Korea, Japan may well have been divided if MacArthur had not defined the goals of the Occupation as he did.

One reason why MacArthur could generate such focus in his followers was that he himself would not compromise the definition of victory. Finally, MacArthur was highly effective at the work of leading his followers to victory. As we will see in the coming lessons, he had the ability to inculcate the *will to win* in his subordinates.

MacArthur articulated this ability to William Ganoe, his chief of staff at West Point, after listening to a professor attempt to reframe a loss by the football team as a victory, given the circumstances of the game. "Chief," he told Ganoe, "you can't stretch defeat into victory by rhetoric. You've got to earn it by downright achievement. You've got to have that spirit behind, that will to win, that self-abnegation to sacrifice up to your capability, no matter what the odds. Even a tie is a defeat."

The clarity of MacArthur's focus on victory remained intact until the end of his life. In 1962, during his final speech at West Point, he described the momentous changes that were taking place in the world and told the cadets:

> *And through all this welter of change and development, your mission remains fixed, determined, inviolable—it is to win our wars. Everything else in your professional career is but a corollary to this vital dedication. All other public purpose, all other public projects, all other public needs, great or small, will find others for their accomplishment; but you are the ones who are trained to fight; yours is the profession of arms…*

"In war, indeed, there is no substitute for victory."

Reflection Questions:

- How is victory defined in your organization?

- Are you communicating the will to win to your followers?

Chapter 4

Understand the Situation

Strategy can be informed by generic and proven principles, but it cannot depend on those principles alone. The environment in which an organization is operating must also inform strategy. In short, leaders cannot create successful strategies in a vacuum.

MacArthur demonstrated his understanding of this principle early in his career, when he was a staff officer in WWI. In France, MacArthur quickly gained a reputation as a frontline leader, but it wasn't just bravado that drove him to expose himself to danger. Here is how he described his first contact with enemy troops on February 26, 1918:

> *I had long felt it was imperative to know by personal observation what the division had to face. It is all very well to make a perfect plan of attack, to work out in theory a foolproof design for victory. But if the plan does not consider the caliber of the troops, the terrain to be fought over, the enemy strength opposed, then it may become confused and fail. I went to see General de Bazelaire, but he was reluctant to authorize me to join a French raiding party out to capture Boche prisoners. I told him frankly, "I cannot fight them if I cannot see them." He understood, and told me to go.*

Later in his career, as MacArthur advanced to higher levels of command, his ability to gain firsthand intelligence was naturally constrained. But the intelligence function always remained a priority in his headquarters. In WWII, as commander in the southwest Pacific, MacArthur refused repeated offers of covert assistance from William "Wild Bill" Donovan and the fledgling Office of Strategic Services (OSS), the precursor of the CIA. He had established his own intelligence staff and preferred the immediacy and control of having it operate under his command.

After arriving in Australia and finding only minimal intelligence resources, MacArthur authorized the establishment of a variety of operations. The Allied Translator and Interpreter Section was one of the most extensive. It grew to 4,000 interpreters and translators, who interrogated more than 14,000 Japanese prisoners of war and translated more than 20 million pages of enemy documents. The Allied Intelligence Bureau ran more than 250 covert missions behind enemy lines. The Allied Geographical Section created almost 200,000 terrain studies, handbooks, and special reports that informed MacArthur's combat operations in headquarters as well in the field, and the Central Bureau broke Japanese codes and deciphered enemy messages.

MacArthur also made extensive use of the Australian Coast Watching Service. The Coast Watchers network, which was established in September 1939, consisted of "jungle-wise gold miners, copra traders and planters, missionaries, telegraph operators, and administrative officials" who, alone or in very small groups, remained behind in Japanese-occupied territories to report enemy activity via radio or any way they could. In 1950, MacArthur acknowledged their information and their sacrifices, saying, "They are officially credited with having been a crucial and deciding factor in the Allied victories of Guadalcanal and Tulagi, and later on in the operations of New Britain, especially in the landing and seizure of the Cape Gloucester area."

The degree to which MacArthur's island campaigns depended on intelligence was not widely known until classified documents were released decades after the war. For instance, he gained a tremendous source of information when, after the Battle of the Bismarck Sea, a lifeboat full of Japanese documents was found on Goodenough Island. The Allied Translator and Interpreter Service discovered that it contained a listing of 40,000 officers in the Japanese Army and used it to ascertain the locations and strengths of enemy units throughout the Pacific. In turn, MacArthur used this data to great advantage when creating the brilliant bypassing operations (see Chapter 9) for which he became justly famous.

In fact, the Battle of the Bismarck Sea was precipitated by the breaking of the Japanese Army Water Transport code. In late February 1943, the interception and decoding of an enemy order alerted MacArthur's headquarters to the movement of a large troop convoy aimed at reinforcing enemy positions in New Guinea. Reconnaissance planes located the convoy, and on March 3, MacArthur's air forces (under command of General George Kenney) attacked the convoy. There were practically no Allied losses. The actual numbers have been long disputed, but it appears that all but a few of the ships were destroyed, and several thousand enemy troops died.

MacArthur's use of intelligence was not restricted to warfare or to the disposition of the enemy alone. Leaders also need to know what is going on in their organizations. While Superintendent at West Point, he asked Chief of Staff Ganoe the following:

> *Chief, do you know what "P.R." stands for? It's personal reconnaissance. Any commander in the field would be derelict, to the point of murder, if he didn't know firsthand how his units were disposed, how the weapons were emplaced, exactly where his left and right were—in fact, every detail he could scrutinize. Why shouldn't such detailed reconnaissance apply to a higher institution of learning?*

"I cannot fight them if I cannot see them."

Reflection Questions:

- Do you fall into the trap of creating strategy in a vacuum?

- What sources of competitive and market intelligence can you tap into to better inform your organization's strategic planning process?

Chapter 5

Use Every Available Means

Strategies that are bound by the constraints of the past and the limitations of the present are often doomed to failure. Great leaders envision unbounded leaps from the present into the future and then apply all of their creativity and resourcefulness to enable those leaps. As MacArthur advised, they use "every available means" to achieve victory.

MacArthur emerged from WWI, a watershed in the history of warfare, with this principle firmly in mind. He had witnessed the death and destruction that resulted when military leaders attempted to apply traditional methods to a new kind of war. In 1920, he wrote from West Point:

> *War had become a phenomenon which truly involved the nation in arms...The great numbers involved made it impossible to apply the old rigid methods which had been so successful when battle lines were not so extensive. The rule of this war can but apply to that of the future. Improvisation will be the watchword.*

In the southwest Pacific in WWII, the "old rigid methods" were particularly limiting. MacArthur's goal was to drive from Australia back to Philippines. The area between the two points was roughly the size of the continental United States and comprised of island stepping stones. Further, for many months, the difficulty of MacArthur's task was exacerbated by severe shortages of troops and equipment.

It was this challenge that forced MacArthur to consider how to best use every means at his disposal to attain victory. One of the notable results was the "triphibious" concept, in which ground, sea, and air forces were combined in tightly integrated strategic plans. In Japan after the war, MacArthur declared it the source of his success:

> *The victory was a triumph for the concept of the complete integration of the three dimensions of war—ground, sea, and air. By a thorough use of each arm in conjunction with the corresponding utilization of the other two, the enemy was reduced to a condition of helplessness...*
>
> *The great lesson for the future is that success in the art of war depends upon a complete integration of the services. In unity will lie military strength. We cannot win with only backs and ends, and no line however strong can go alone. Victory will rest with the team.*

The triphibious concept not only enabled MacArthur to leap and envelop enemy strongholds; it enabled him to stretch the theater's limited resources. As MacArthur took the offensive in New Guinea in late 1942, he could not muster enough ships to transport the troops and equipment needed to attack the Japanese on the northeastern coast, and the Owen Stanley Range blocked large-scale land transport. So, MacArthur turned to General George Kenney and the Air Force for logistical support.

Working with artillerymen, Kenney's airmen figured out how to disassemble, load, and deliver big guns to battle. Kenney described an early test of the process:

> *The next day, a B-17 landed at Seven Mile Airdrome carrying a 105-mm. howitzer, a tractor to pull it with, the gun crew of eight men, fifty rounds of ammunition, a tool kit, and the camouflage net to shield it from the eyes of Jap aviators. General MacArthur went down with me to see the gun unloaded. His grin was worth the work of getting it up here. How they ever stuffed that 10,000 pounds of gun, ammunition, crew, and miscellaneous equipment into that B-17 I don't know, but they went back to Brisbane that night to get the other three guns of the battery. The next morning, two DC-3s took the pieces of gun Number One to Dobodura, where they were reassembled and put into action. By this time, the ground troops and General MacArthur decided we could haul anything in an airplane.*

When paratroopers were used to capture Nadzab (also on New Guinea), Kenney delivered artillery by parachute, too:

> *[Australian General] Vasey said he had no doubt that our preparatory strafing attack on Nadzab would remove all the opposition, but he would like to have some artillery on hand to assist the paratroopers when they landed. I told him to give us one of the guns to play with and we would see if we could drop the main parts by parachute without damaging them. That afternoon, after several practice drops, the scheme looked feasible, so we added an Australian 25-pounder gun battery to the parachute show.*

This innovative use of air support drew widespread attention. In February 16, 1943, Winston Churchill wired this to MacArthur: "I have watched with particular admiration your masterly employment of transport aircraft to solve most complicated and diverse logistical problems."

The employment of every available means to achieve strategic goals was a MacArthur trademark throughout WWII. New tactics were created so that light and medium tanks could be used in the Pacific jungles. New bombing techniques and equipment enabled low-level and "skip-bombing." Even Charles Lindbergh lent a hand. In 1944, MacArthur and Kenney waylaid the long-distance aviator during a fact-finding mission and enlisted his help in increasing the range of their P-38 fighters. Lindbergh taught them how to increase the plane's range from 400 miles to as much as 850 miles, and he enabled operations such as the October 1944 bombing raid on the enemy-held oil refineries at Balikpapan, Borneo, which provided 40 percent of the lubricating oil needed by the Japanese.

"Improvisation will be the watchword."

Reflection Questions:

- Are your strategic plans unnecessarily limited by beliefs and/or circumstances?

- How can you adapt your organization's existing resources to better serve your goals?

Chapter 6

Manage the Environment

All organizations are part of a larger environment—a market or an economy or a military theater. The organization's capability to operate within that environment is a primary determinant of its success. Leaders are responsible for understanding and maximizing that capability.

MacArthur understood that the environment in which an organization operates is "neutral"; that is, it does not inherently favor any one competitor over another. But he also knew that the environment offered powerful advantages to the leader and organization that could best adapt to it.

In WWII, MacArthur's first job was to adapt his own forces to the environment. For instance, disease was a major problem in Papua New Guinea. Former Secretary of Defense Caspar Weinberger, who served as an infantry officer there, says, "Seventy percent of our unit came down with malaria. I was one of them. We didn't even know how to deal with it in the beginning. We would have been quite unable to carry out any kind of combat had the Japanese attacked."

Realizing the toll that malaria was taking on his forces, MacArthur established the Combined Advisory Committee on Tropical Medicine, Hygiene and Sanitation in early 1943. It was a group of Australian and American medical experts who created strategies for combating disease and began a large-scale prevention program. In less than 15 months, the malaria rate was reduced by 95 percent. MacArthur later wrote:

On the Papuan front, [the malaria mosquito] had been responsible for more non-effectives than any other single factor. But we finally conquered this ever-present menace...The Japanese efforts along these lines were ineffective and their losses assumed enormous proportions. Nature is neutral in war, but if you can beat it and the enemy does not, it becomes a powerful ally.

That is exactly what MacArthur did in the Pacific. He took positions far behind the Japanese strongholds and forced them to fight the jungle before they could fight him. Here is how Robert White, who reported to MacArthur's headquarters in August 1942, described the result:

[MacArthur] said, "Let's make the jungle our allies much as we can." So, throughout the rest of the war, we always landed where the Japanese weren't. [We] set up our own perimeters, let the Japanese live out in the jungle...and let him have to move hundreds of miles up through the jungle to get to us and by the time they got to us...they looked like they came out of a deep hole in the ground. It's just the way we thought of them; they were emaciated, sick, ill; the jungle was an ally for us in those conditions.

The weather was another key environmental factor in the Pacific, and MacArthur ran afoul of it during the invasion of Leyte. Correspondent William Dunn explained:

What neither the guerrillas nor our meteorologists could tell us was that the monsoon season, which we anticipated and believed we were prepared for, would be a record-smasher, bringing with it two typhoons (a third was a near-miss) and torrential rains that would pour some 50 inches—more than four feet of water on this combat zone in ten weeks...Such conditions explain why it took us a little more than 2 weeks to capture 85 percent of the island but almost 2 months to secure the remaining 15 percent.

Typically, however, MacArthur tried his best to enlist the weather in the Allied effort. In the invasion at Lae, New Guinea, for example, the landing date was kept flexible so that it could take place on (as George Kenney remembered it) "a day when the fog in the Vitiaz Straits area was so thick that the Jap airplanes from Rabaul could not get through to interfere with our shipping."

MacArthur also used the topography of the Pacific islands in the same manner. He utilized this principle of strategy when planning the defense of the Philippines in the late 1930s:

[G]eography did not cease its defensive favors to the Philippines when it made them an isolated group. Nature has studded these islands with mountainous formations, making practicable landing places for large forces extremely few in number and difficult in character. The vital area of Luzon, in which dwell approximately seven million Filipinos, presents in all its long shoreline only two coastal regions in which a hostile army of any size could land. Each of these is broken by strong defensive positions, which if properly manned and prepared would present to any attacking force a practically impossible problem of penetration.

But nature has still further endowed the Philippines with defensive possibilities: 60 percent of the national terrain consists of great forest areas, impenetrable by powerful military units. The mountainous terrain, the primeval forests, and the lack of communications combine to create a theater of operations in which a defensive force of only moderate efficiency and strength could test the capabilities of the most powerful and splendidly equipped army that could be assembled there.

Other islands of the Archipelago possess similar defensive possibilities. In some instances, no practicable landing places for large forces exist. In every case, determined troops at the shoreline could deny landing to an attacker of many times their own number.

MacArthur's conclusion was that the larger of two opponents would always win in equal conditions, but he added, "Equality of conditions never exists in warfare, and war has therefore shown many startling reversals in which the apparently weaker opponent achieved victory."

"Nature...if you can get it on your side and the enemy does not, it becomes a powerful ally."

Reflection Questions:

- What are the principle conditions in the environment in which your organization operates?

- How can you use those conditions to gain an advantage over the competition?

Chapter 7

Utilize Surprise

Surprise is a highly effective weapon in the strategic arsenal and can be a decisive factor in the success of organizational plans. It can confound competitors, undermine their defenses, and relegate them to playing catch-up. It can also delight customers, win their loyalty, and build market share. Smart strategists incorporate the element of surprise in their plans.

The advantage of surprise is a well-established, battle-proven fact of military strategy, so it is no surprise that MacArthur was a firm advocate of the principle. As you've seen, the plan for the Inchon invasion was rooted in the element of surprise. In fact, during the fateful conference that resulted in the operation's approval, MacArthur turned the myriad objections to the plan on their head by appealing to the power of surprise. He said:

> *The very arguments you have made as to the impracticabilities involved will tend to ensure for me the element of surprise. For the enemy commander will reason that no one would be so brash as to make such an attempt. Surprise is the most vital element for success at war.*

MacArthur tried to capture the element of surprise in all his plans. In early 1942, when he began planning his escape from Corregidor, the most obvious mode of transport was a submarine. But MacArthur had a different idea. Admiral Charles Bulkeley, then a PT boat squadron commander, explained:

> *MacArthur was a sheer genius in my books there. And I say this because no one in the whole world would expect him to go out on a PT boat, a motor torpedo boat to make a break out. Ah, it just seemed so foreign.*
>
> *The motor torpedo boats or PT boats were used because MacArthur decided that [was] the one and only way he could achieve complete surprise with Japanese forces which were surrounding him and intending to capture him. [I]t's the genius of the man that no one ever expect that the torpedo boats would make a break out and carry MacArthur and his principle generals as well as his wife and child...And the Japanese have...twenty-two to twenty-seven ships outside the bay. They had floating mines...we had mine fields. It was a very dangerous thing to go out of that bay, look out of that harbor and no one ever expected it.*

Late in the war, as Allied troops were descending on Manila, MacArthur used the element of surprise to liberate almost 4,000 prisoners being held in Santo Tomás University. Knowing that the Japanese had been killing prisoners of war, MacArthur instructed General Vernon Mudge, commander of the 1st Cavalry, located at Giumba, north of Manila, "Go to Manila. Go around the Nips, bounce off the Nips, but go to Manila. Free the internees at Santo Thomás."

Correspondent William Dunn described the ensuing operation:

> *Nowhere else in the history of warfare will you find an instance of a military commander sending a force of barely eight hundred men into a city of more than a million population known to be held by the equivalent of at least two divisions of infantry. It was impossible, and the Japanese knew it was impossible. That was the premise on which MacArthur founded his entire strategy for the thrust. Based on his long association with the Oriental and his study of this particular Oriental, he was sure the Japanese would mark the progress of this fragile column and, from the very first, not believe what they saw.*

The enemy troops did stand by in amazement as the 1st Cavalry made its run through the city. By the time the Japanese responded, the camp was taken and the 37th Infantry had entered the city to secure the position.

Finally, it is important to note that MacArthur did not simply conceive a plan based on surprise and leave its success to the fates. He frequently used feints and other deceptions to disguise his intent. In preparing for the invasion of Hollandia in New Guinea, the 5th Air Force bombed the more likely targets of Hansa Bay and Wewak as often as Hollandia itself. PT boat raids were made, dummy parachutes were dropped, "covert" missions were purposely seen, and submarines released life rafts at the alternative targets. MacArthur explained:

> *Comprehensive deception plans were put into effect to further the enemy's belief that the attack would fall on Wewak and Hansa Bay. He strengthened these positions to the neglect of the real points of attack.*

On April 22, 1944, the invasion of Hollandia began. In four days, the area had been successfully secured. Just under 160 Americans died; 3,300 Japanese were killed. Another 7,000 enemy troops were forced to flee 140 miles through the jungle to the nearest Japanese base. Nature took over at that point; only 1,000 men survived the trek.

"In war, surprise is decisive."

Reflection Questions:

- What do your competitors expect you to do next?

- Can you act contrary to expectations to achieve your organization's goals?

Chapter 8

Multiply Your Rate of Movement

The need for speed in organizational movement and response has been widely acknowledged in the past decade. Lumbering corporate giants have either stagnated or disappeared from the business scene. Sleek, fast-moving companies that are able to stay ahead of changes in society and technology have dominated many markets. Leaders in successful organizations have embraced MacArthur's dictum: Multiply your rate of movement.

MacArthur was preaching the speed creed 70 years before it became a major factor in strategic success. In 1935, as the Army Chief of Staff, he strenuously argued for increased mobility. He wrote:

> *The protective power of modern weapons is so great that where these are strongly and deliberately organized for defense they practically assure invulnerability. Only through surprise action can collision with the enemy's prepared positions be avoided, and to gain surprise nothing is more important than superiority in mobility. The constant trend in the modern world is toward greater and greater speed. Any army that fails to keep in step with this trend is, far from making necessary progress toward modernization, going steadily and irrevocably backward.*

To MacArthur, every element of the Army's effort had to be enlisted in the drive for greater speed. He said:

> *Tactical organization must, of course, be such as to produce the essential qualities of mobility and fire power. Nothing is more important to the effectiveness of an army than an ability to move rapidly. A law of physics that applies equally to warfare is that while striking force increases directly with the mass applied, it increases according to the square of the speed of the application. Through proper organization in all echelons, through the development and perfection of reliable combat units capable of speedy maneuver, and through the improvement of transportation, maintenance, communication and supply arrangements, the objective of maximum speed must be pursued. These truisms apply to all armies...*

The utilization of technology was a key element in MacArthur's effort to increase the Army's rate of movement. Although he was severely constrained by the budget cuts of the Depression years, he advised mobility through the mechanization of cavalry, artillery, and infantry units. "[N]othing is more important to the future efficiency of the Army than to multiply its rate of movement." Toward that end, MacArthur supported the expansion of tank and mechanized supply forces. He also advocated the expansion of military air power, saying, "Foremost among these units in point of speed and flexibility of movement is the air force."

During WWII, MacArthur was still preaching speed in strategic execution. In late 1942, he changed commanders in Papua, New Guinea when the Army bogged down at Buna. When his new commander, General Robert Eichelberger, did not seem to be moving quickly enough, MacArthur told him:

> *Time is fleeting and our dangers increasing with its passage. However admirable individual acts of courage may be; however important administrative functions may seem; however splendid and electrical your presence has proven, remember that your mission is to take Buna. All other things are merely subsidiary to this. No alchemy is going to produce this for you; it can only be done in battle and sooner or later this battle must be engaged. Hasten your preparations and when you are ready—strike, for as I have said, time is working desperately against us.*

In his drive to Manila during the retaking of the Luzon in 1945, MacArthur acted, as well as commanded, to increase the speed of the attack. Frustrated by General Walter Krueger's cautious and slow progress with the 6th Army, MacArthur set up his own headquarters 50 miles closer to Manila than Krueger. Over the objections of his staff, he took to touring the frontlines of the advance in his jeep, prodding the troops to move faster by his own example. He also peppered Krueger with messages, such as this one on January 30, "There was a noticeable lack of drive and aggressive initiative today in the movement toward Calumpit."

In the end, MacArthur ordered three different units to enter Manila, setting off a race to determine which would capture the honor of being first. Afterward, Lord Mountbatten, the commander of the Southeast Asia Theater, wrote MacArthur, "The speed of your advance on Manila and the capture of the town were astonishing..."

MacArthur offered some final words of warning for those who ignore the need for speed:

> *The history of failure in war can almost be summed up in two words: Too Late. Too late in comprehending the deadly purpose of a potential enemy; too late in realizing the mortal danger; too late in preparedness; too late in uniting all possible forces for resistance; too late in standing with one's friends.*

"Even the Lord, Himself, cannot save those who do not move fast."

Reflection Questions:

- Can you extend the profit lifecycle of your products and services by bringing them more quickly to market?

- How can you create a sense of urgency within your organization?

Chapter 9

Hit 'em Where They Ain't

Organizational success depends on the ability to enter and capture new markets. But few organizations enjoy uncontested access to the markets, and the very nature of capitalism guarantees that profitable markets will quickly become highly competitive. Smart leaders eschew head-to-head market competition for creative strategies that take full advantage of their strengths and their opponents' weaknesses.

In WWII, MacArthur utilized exactly such a strategy to great effect in the southwest Pacific. He called it by several names: "hit 'em where they ain't," "leap-frogging," and "bypassing." Elegant in its simplicity, in essence, MacArthur refused to attack enemy strongholds. Instead, he leapt beyond them to less-well-defended spots and then either destroyed them in an envelopment or (in the case of the Japanese island strongholds) simply cut their communications and supplies and left them behind while he drove forward. MacArthur described the strategy as growing naturally from "three-dimensional warfare—the triphibious concept." He said:

> *It was the practical application of this system of warfare—to avoid frontal attack with its terrible loss of life; to bypass Japanese strong points and neutralize them by cutting their lines of supply; to thus isolate their armies and starve them on the battlefield; to, as [baseball hall of famer Wee] Willie Keeler used to say, "hit 'em where they ain't"—that from this time forward guided my movements and operations.*

MacArthur did not originate the strategy, but he quickly realized that head-to-head combat was not feasible in the Pacific. In a September 21, 1943 press release, he explained:

> *This is the very opposite of what is termed "island hopping" which is the gradual pushing back of the enemy by direct frontal pressure with the consequent heavy casualties which will certainly be involved. Key points must of course be taken but a wise choice of such will obviate the need for storming the mass of islands now in enemy possession. "Island hopping" with extravagant losses and slow progress—some press reports indicating victory postponed as late as 1949—is not my idea of how to end the war as soon and as cheaply as possible. New conditions require for solution, and new weapons require for maximum application, new and imaginative methods. Wars are never won in the past.*

MacArthur became the strongest proponent and most-skilled adopter of the "hit 'em where they ain't" concept after the Joint Chiefs insisted that he bypass the Japanese stronghold at Rabaul on the island of New Britain. It was in discussing that strategy that MacArthur aide Sid Huff first heard him articulate it:

> *One of the conferees estimated that a successful attack on Rabaul, for example, would require a far greater Allied force and would cost more casualties than had the Battle of Guadalcanal. The air experts pointed out that a great many more planes than were available would be needed. And where were we going to get the planes or the ships or the extra divisions? Furthermore, Rabaul was only a beginning. Beyond Rabaul lay other enemy bases just as formidable.*
>
> *MacArthur had been sitting back in his chair, listening and smoking a cigarette, but saying nothing. Now he leaned forward as one of the conferees remarked, "I don't see how we can take these strong points with our limited forces."*
>
> *"Well," the General said, in a slow, deliberate voice, "let's just say we won't take them." He tapped his cigarette nonchalantly against the edge of an ashtray. "In fact, gentlemen, I don't want them!"*
>
> *...The idea was simple, but it was unorthodox and, in the beginning, there was opposition by a number of MacArthur's advisers, who felt that each enemy position had to be destroyed as we advanced. In his familiar fashion the General ignored such timidity, hit the enemy where he was weakest, bypassed his strong points, which were then isolated and bombarded and left to die on the vine.*

In fact, Rabaul was never invaded. Instead, between December 1943 and April 1944, it was isolated along with 140,000 Japanese troops in a series of low-cost, "hit 'em where they ain't" operations. By the end of the war, several million Japanese soldiers had been stranded throughout the Pacific. After the war, Japanese staff officer Colonel Matsuichi Juio said:

> *...this was the type of strategy that we hated most. The Americans attacked and seized with minimum losses, a relatively weak area, constructed air fields, and then proceeded to cut the supply lines to our troops in that area. Our strong points were gradually starved out. The Japanese Army preferred direct assault after the German fashion, but the Americans flowed into weaker points, and submerged us, just as water seeks the weakest entry to sink a ship.*

"Bastion after bastion, considered by [the Japanese Army] impregnable and barring our way, had been by-passed and rendered impotent and useless..."

Reflection Questions:

- In what segments of your markets are your competitors most vulnerable?

- How can you use the "hit 'em where they ain't" strategy to gain a secure foothold in a new market?

Chapter 10

Aim for Envelopment

"Hitting 'em where they ain't" offers an economical method for establishing a foothold in the market, but its greatest value is as a supporting move in the larger strategic goal of envelopment. *Envelopment* is the process of encircling a target, be it an enemy army or an economic market, and capturing it. Great leaders focus on driving toward strategic envelopments.

MacArthur used the "hit 'em where they ain't" (or "leap-frogging") concept to economically accomplish the flanking moves needed to envelop and destroy his opponents:

> *The system was popularly called "leap-frogging," and was hailed as something new in warfare. But it was actually the adaptation of modern instrumentalities of war to a concept as ancient as war itself. Derived from the classic strategy of envelopment, it was given a new name, imposed by modern conditions.*

In fact, MacArthur's entire line of attack in WWII, which extended from his secure anchor in Australia through New Guinea and the Philippine Islands and ultimately aimed at Japan itself, was conceived as a series of continuous envelopments. Here is how MacArthur's intelligence chief General Charles Willoughby described it:

[L]acking the facilities to fight the Japanese head-on, he proposed no frontal strokes at Japanese strong points. What he sought for each individual battle was the opportunity to get around and behind the enemy, striking him obliquely on the flank and grappling for his supply lines. The whole MacArthur theory of maneuver was a hark-back past the man-devouring frontal assaults of World War I to the fluidity of Napoleonic times.

Thus, the 500-mile leap up the New Guinea coastline to Hollandia was conceived of as an envelopment within an envelopment. The first envelopment was the invasion of Hollandia itself. On April 22, 1944, the operation began with two simultaneous landings to the east and west of the target, 30 miles apart. The western force executed a double envelopment, leaving the Japanese no recourse but to either fight a losing battle or to slip away into the jungle.

Once secured, Hollandia became the final element in a much larger envelopment covering the entire 500 miles of MacArthur's strategic leap. MacArthur explained:

The operation throws a loop of envelopment around the enemy's 18th Army, dispersed along the coast of New Guinea in the Madang, Alixshafen, Hansa Bay, Wewak sectors, similar to the Solomons and Bismarck loops of envelopment. To the east are the Australians and Americans; to the west are the Americans; to the north the sea controlled by our Allied naval forces; to the south untraversed jungle mountain ranges; and over all our Allied air mastery. The enemy army is now completely isolated.

MacArthur repeated this pattern of envelopment again and again. In addition to traditional land-based single and double envelopments, he used the Airborne's parachute troops to create vertical envelopments and attacked by sea to establish amphibious envelopments. After the war, he described the effectiveness:

In war the complete blockade of a force dependent for food and other supply from outside sources is the most effective weapon known to military science. It was through the use of this weapon that our starving men on Bataan and Corregidor were finally forced to yield to the enemy hordes who surrounded them. It was through the use of this same weapon, more than any other, that the Japanese armed forces were finally brought to the futility of further resistance, as segment after segment of their extended positions, by envelopment, were cut off from needed supplies on the grim road back. Thereafter, when reconquest of the Philippines completely severed the Japanese war-gained Empire and permitted a blockade of the Japanese home islands themselves, traditionally dependent for sustenance from sources without, total collapse became imminent.

One last point for those planning to use the envelopment strategy: the ability to close the loop around a market or an opponent is critical to the strategy's success. This was why MacArthur insisted on Inchon in his plan to destroy the North Korean Army via amphibious envelopment. Kunsan, a port 100 miles south of Inchon, was much closer to the Pusan Perimeter and did not feature as many natural hazards. It was favored by several of those who felt that Inchon was too risky, but MacArthur rejected the idea. He said:

It would be an attempted envelopment which would not envelop. It would not sever or destroy the enemy's supply lines or distribution center, and would therefore serve little purpose. It would be a "short envelopment," and nothing in war is more futile. Better no flank movement than one such as this...The enemy will merely roll back on his lines of supply and communication.

"It has always proved the ideal method for success by inferior in number but faster moving troops."

Reflection Questions:

- Can you effectively capture your main market by enveloping a competitor's position?

- Which of your market positions are vulnerable to envelopment?

Chapter 11

Concentrate Your Force

The successful execution of a strategy requires the application of the right amount of effort at the right time in the right place. In military terms, this is known as *concentration of force* or the *principle of mass.* Great leaders know how, when, and where to concentrate the organizational force at their disposal.

MacArthur deftly applied the principle of mass throughout his military campaigns. This does not mean that he committed all his resources in every situation. On the contrary, he often attacked successfully with much smaller forces and fewer resources than his opponents enjoyed. One notable example was his return to the Philippines at Leyte. In describing the Leyte invasion fleet, MacArthur said:

> *On the waters around me lay one of the greatest armadas in history...Altogether, there were 700 of these ships of war. They carried 174,000 of America's finest fighting men, veteran soldiers now a match for any warrior the world has ever known. The size of the landing force was equal to about half the Japanese strength in the islands, but the enemy was scattered. My force was concentrated. I intended my maneuver and surprise to bring superior force to bear at the points of actual combat and, thereby, destroy him piecemeal.*

The Japanese also saw Leyte as an opportunity to crush their opponent. Two days after MacArthur waded ashore on October 20, 1944, Japanese Southern Army commander Hisaichi Terauchi ordered that every resource be committed to "totally destroy the enemy on Leyte."

Terauchi's order set in motion exactly the same "piecemeal" application of force that MacArthur had expected. As the Japanese committed reinforcements in incremental numbers, the battle for the island stretched through December. But the Japanese never massed enough force to stop MacArthur. Finally, on December 25, General Yamashita announced that no more men could be spared for Leyte. Cut off, the Japanese troops already on the island fought on until May; 27,000 of them died. The American death toll was 700 men.

MacArthur's understanding of the principle of concentration of force trumped superior Japanese forces on many other occasions. And when the concentration of force was not in his favor, he did not fight. Instead, as we've seen, MacArthur leap-frogged to a point where his concentration of force was favorable and enveloped the enemy. In WWII, he could then let George Kenney's air force and the jungle take their toll.

When conflict with a superior concentration of force is unavoidable, the only possible response is to create the necessary mass as quickly as possible. MacArthur was confronted with this situation at the outbreak of the Korean War and before the counterstroke at Inchon. Unprepared to fight, but forced to either engage the North Koreans or be pushed off the peninsula completely, MacArthur found himself in the position of committing forces in a piecemeal fashion. He later said:

> *I threw in troops by air in the hope of establishing a locus of resistance around which I could rally the fast-retreating South Korean forces. I had hoped by that arrogant display of strength to fool the enemy into a belief that I had greater resources at my disposal than I did. We gained ten days by this process…*

That gave MacArthur enough time to fly in the 24th Division, but the concentration of force was still against him. As the 24th fought a bitter delaying action, he brought the 8th Army into South Korea and called the Joint Chiefs of Staff for reinforcements. By the end of August, the concentrations of force were approximately equal, and the North Koreans had been stopped at the Pusan Perimeter. MacArthur had traded space and men for the time needed to mass a force equal to his opponents.

Equal forces, however, are also undesirable. Throughout this same period, MacArthur was aggressively advocating a "hit 'em where they ain't" envelopment. He argued:

> *The only alternative to a stroke such as I propose will be the continuation of the savage sacrifice we are making at Pusan, with no hope of relief in sight. Are you content to let our troops stay in that bloody perimeter like beef cattle in a slaughterhouse? Who will take responsibility for such a tragedy? Certainly, I will not.*

Three weeks later, MacArthur turned the tide of the war when he brought a greater concentration of force to bear on the North Korean Army at Inchon.

"My force was concentrated."

Reflection Questions:

- Are your organization's resources and efforts properly concentrated among its various goals?

- Have you applied the right force at the right time and place to achieve your primary goal?

Chapter 12

Build in Flexibility

In part, strategic plans are based on predictions about the future. Marketing plans, for instance, seek to anticipate the reactions of customers and competitors. But predictions are rarely exact reflections of the future reality, so smart leaders prepare themselves to be unprepared. They avoid the two most common traps of planning: inflexibility and over-planning.

MacArthur received a dramatic lesson in the disadvantages of over-reliance on a plan during the St. Mihiel Offensive in WWI. The fight should have been a difficult one, but realizing that they were heavily out-numbered, the Germans unexpectedly began evacuating their positions before the attack began on September 12, 1918. MacArthur's 84th Brigade quickly cut through the light resistance of the remaining enemy units, and by the end of the second day, the brigade had already achieved its final objective of the operation.

That night, MacArthur undertook a personal reconnaissance and realized that the fast advance had exposed the German stronghold in the fortified city of Metz. He concluded:

> *Here was an unparalleled opportunity to break the Hindenburg Line at its pivotal point. There it lay, our prize wide open for the taking. Take it and we would be in an excellent position to cut off south Germany from the rest of the country; it would lead to the invasion of central Germany by way of*

the practically undefended Moselle Valley. Victory at Metz would cut the great lines of communication and supply behind the German front, and might bring the war to a quick close.

MacArthur reported the opportunity to the divisional chief of staff and asked for permission to attack. It was rejected because Metz was not an objective in the strategic plan. MacArthur appealed the decision to both the corps and army commands and was rejected by both. He later said:

Had we seized this unexpected opportunity we would have saved thousands of American lives lost in the dim recesses of the Argonne Forest. It was an example of the inflexibility in the pursuit of previously conceived ideas that is, unfortunately, too frequent in modern warfare.

It was a lesson that MacArthur learned well. During WWII, where MacArthur was in command, two or three sets of plans encompassing alternative strategies were often prepared in advance of major campaigns. He was also quick to discard his own plans when unexpected opportunities arose. When General Kenney reported that Los Negros in the Admiralty Islands was vulnerable, MacArthur immediately ordered that the invasion schedule be moved up a month and a new plan be prepared for an invasion four days hence.

MacArthur's return to the Philippines occurred more than two months early, and at Leyte instead of Mindanao, after the Navy reported that the central Philippines appeared to be only lightly defended. General William Ritchie, who witnessed the speed of this major decision, said,

[MacArthur had] one of the finest strategical and tactical minds we ever had in the military history of this country. He had vision; he could visualize an entire operation, while at the same time he could fit in all the tactical plans to make that operation come out. He also had the ability to shift the overall plan to the breaks that come into it.

MacArthur also avoided the trap of over-planning and the action paralysis that often accompanies it. He disliked the fact that "[f]inal decisions are made not at the front by those who are there, but many miles away by those who can but guess at the possibilities and potentialities. The essence of victory lies in the answer to where and when."

This is why MacArthur built as much flexibility into his plans as possible. He attributed the speed of the initial drive on Luzon, the last great battle of the Pacific war, to this flexibility. He explained:

> *There was no fixed timetable. I hoped to proceed as rapidly as possible, especially as time was an element connected with the release of our prisoners. I have always felt, however, that to endeavor to formulate in advance details of a campaign is hazardous, as it tends to warp the judgment of a commander when faced with unexpected conditions brought about by the uncertainties of enemy reaction or enemy initiative. I therefore never attempted fixed dates for anything but the start of operations…No greater danger can confront a field commander than too-close "back seat driving" and too-rigid "timetables" of operations from those above. There is natural limit on a command, due to its inherent strengths and weaknesses which place a bracket upon its operations, which only its own commander can know and which even he at times has to estimate. Any arbitrary violation either way by those not present in the theater of operations might well prove disastrous.*

"I have always felt, however, that to endeavor to formulate in advance details of a campaign is hazardous..."

Reflection Questions:

- Do your plans reflect the line between strategy and tactics?

- Are your strategies flexible enough to account for the unpredictability of the environment in which they will be executed?

Chapter 13

Make a "Reconnaissance in Force"

The most rewarding strategies are often those that are bold and original. But by their very nature, they also tend to be risk-laden. That is when smart leaders turn to the *reconnaissance in force*, a military tactic that can lessen the odds of failure by reducing the unknown factors that exist in a plan without putting their entire investment at risk.

The concept of committing a small force aimed at identifying the actual situation immediately before risking his main force served MacArthur in several ways. He could probe and test the position and strength of his opponents. He retained the advantages of surprise and flexibility of response. And he could reframe risky operations in more positive light.

MacArthur may well have first learned how to use reconnaissance in force from his father, whose own experiences with the technique as an officer in the 24th Wisconsin during Sherman's drive to Atlanta in the Civil War became a textbook example. Colonel A.L. Wagner, author of *Service of Security and Information*, wrote:

> *The men of this regiment were instructed each to select a tree about 50 yards in front of the line and at command to run forward and halt behind the tree selected. The regiment thus pushing forward by a series of rushes, advanced three-quarters of the distance separating it from the enemy, developed his position and completely gained the object of the reconnaissance, with the loss of only two men killed and eleven wounded.*

His son, in the southwest Pacific in WWII, utilized the technique on a much broader scale. MacArthur conceived the entire operation at Los Negros in the Admiralty Islands as a reconnaissance in force. He told staff physician Roger Egeberg, "Doc, this is a finesse, a reconnaissance in force. Some people think there are 5,000 Japs there, but we will save six months if the operation works." In response to reports that Japanese defenses were light, MacArthur landed 1,000 troops on the beach and went ashore himself to ascertain the situation. Convinced that the position could be held, he ordered the operation expanded to a full-scale invasion. (See Chapter 50.)

MacArthur later explained his plan:

> *My aim was to strike swiftly, achieve surprise, and thus avoid bitter fighting and heavy casualties at the beachhead. If an initial foothold could be established without undue losses, the reconnaissance force would then advance, seize Momote airstrip nearby, and be promptly reinforced. If unforeseen enemy strength should be encountered at the beaches, however, and an unforeseen situation should develop, a speedy withdrawal would be made.*

MacArthur also used a reconnaissance in force during the invasion of Luzon. MacArthur's main force came ashore on the beaches of Lingayen in northern Luzon on January 9, 1944. On January 31, one regiment of the 11th Airborne Division landed on the beach at Nasugbu, 45 miles southwest of Manila, to test the enemy defenses in southern Luzon. When the opposition proved light, General Robert Eichelberger, commanding from the *U.S.S. Spencer*, sent the rest of the division ashore with orders to push on to Manila itself. The division reached the outskirts of the city before bogging down against the Japanese defenses at Nichols Field.

In Korea, on the day before the landing at Inchon, MacArthur used six Navy destroyers as a floating reconnaissance in force to ensure clear passage to the landing site. Captain Robert Schelling described it like this:

> *The 300-foot high island of Wolmi-do commanded the harbor entrance. It was judged to be fortified and would have to be reduced before the landings could take place. What guns did it have and where were they located? Six destroyers would be sent in on D-2 day to find out the hard way—draw fire in order to reveal [the] guns' positions and take them out if we could. The nickname later given to our ships for this mission was "Sitting Ducks."*

Our "reconnaissance in force," as it was called, was a gutsy response by the sailors of the Mansfield, De Haven, Lyman K. Swenson, Collett, Gurke, and Henderson, who took their ships into harm's way, really into the unknown, anchored there, and slugged it out toe-to-toe. A young officer in the De Haven's gun director saw through his spotting glass an enemy gun crew getting ready to fire, and beat them to the draw, thus starting the hour-long fray. We found [the] guns and took many of them out. By D-Day the fortifications were reduced so that our Marines could land and do their great job with minimal casualties.

"Doc, this is a finesse, a reconnaissance in force."

Reflection Questions:

- Can you use a reconnaissance in force to hedge your risk in a new strategy?

- Can you use a reconnaissance in force to market-test a new product or service and still maximize your first-to-market advantage?

Chapter 14

Ensure Supply and Support

The successful execution of strategy is critically dependent on supply and support. In war, it is fatal to launch an attack without adequate ammunition and protective support. Likewise, in business, it is futile to fight for an expanded market share for goods and services you cannot produce and/or deliver. Leaders in all types of organizations must consider and ensure adequate supply and support to achieve their objectives.

In a very real sense, the story of the SW Pacific Theater in WWII is one driven by the flow of supply and support. It started with the very outbreak of the war. The attack on Pearl Harbor cut the U.S. supply lines to the Far East and destroyed the naval fleet on which MacArthur was depending for support. The inability of the United States to supply and reinforce MacArthur's forces made the loss of the Philippine Islands inevitable.

After MacArthur reached Australia, the effort to defend the continent by wrenching the offensive from the Japanese in New Guinea became what his staff referred to as a "battle of supply depots." Again, the lack of support from the United States, created mainly by the "Europe First" priorities of the Roosevelt Administration, loomed over MacArthur. It was during this time, while MacArthur was confidently telling the Australians, "My faith in our ultimate victory is invincible," that he privately wondered, "Must I always lead a forlorn hope?"

Australia, however, was not yet besieged by the Japanese, and it contained resources that were not available in the Philippines. MacArthur drew on those resources to supply and support the southwest Pacific forces. He was instrumental, for example, in the creation of a reverse Lend-Lease program, in which Australia provided supplies to the United States. MacArthur's intelligence chief Charles Willoughby explained:

> *In the last six moths of 1942, probably 65 to 70 percent of all supplies consumed by United States forces came from local production and resources. In addition, MacArthur gave to the neighboring Southern Pacific Theater during that critical period a larger tonnage of supplies than the United States shipped to his own area. In effect, therefore—as far as a drain on the United States is concerned—the Southwest Pacific was 100 percent self-sufficient…Eventually things reached a point where some 15 percent of the national income of Australia, and consequently 15 percent of its productive resources, were going to meet United States needs.*

MacArthur was still severely constrained by the lack of support. He told the War Department in August 1943:

> *It is coming to be evident that sustained effort may be impossible in this theater because of lack of mobility which effectively prevents taking advantage of hostile weaknesses developed or successes gained. Each successive operation will be delayed for purposes of concentration, thus allowing the Japanese to reconsolidate ahead of our offensive effort. This results from lack of shipping.*

The lack of naval support, and his lack of control over the existing U.S. naval forces in the Pacific, explains why MacArthur came to rely on and use air power so extensively. Starting in New Guinea, the Army Air Forces played a starring role in MacArthur's strategy. He later explained:

> *The sweep of my forces along New Guinea had been consistently delivered so that each operation would have the full protection of my own land-based air force. Every step forward had been governed by the basic concept of securing airfields no more than 200 to 300 miles apart from which to secure an "air umbrella" over each progressive thrust into the enemy.*

MacArthur held to this principle of support. Even in the Hollandia operation, in which he leapt more than 500 miles up the New Guinea coast, MacArthur planned a simultaneous invasion at the Japanese airfields at Aitape, which were in-between existing U.S. airfields and Hollandia. It provided the air cover that would be needed at Hollandia after the ships borrowed from the Navy for the landing were returned. MacArthur's only notable exception to his air-support rule was at Leyte. After the near disaster that occurred there when the fleet was decoyed away, he vowed never to move without air cover again.

Finally, the strictures of supply and support informed MacArthur's overall strategy for winning the Pacific War. Willoughby said:

> *[It was] a simple yet profound strategical concept; that of an arrow-straight axis of advance from Australia to the Philippines that would result in severing the Japanese supply lines from the oil, rubber, tin, and rice of the Indies, Indo-China, and Malaya. MacArthur held to this economical view of strategy...*"

"We are doing what we can with what we have."

Reflection Questions:

- Is your organization's supply chain constricting your performance?

- Are the supply and support requirements of your strategic plan fully considered?

Chapter 15

Be Aggressive in Defense

At one time or another, organizations inevitably find themselves in a defensive position. Perhaps their markets and/or customer base come under competitive attack or (in the case of the military) their nation and/or allies are invaded. No matter what the circumstances, great leaders understand that the only effective defense is an aggressive defense.

MacArthur never relished being forced into a defensive position, and he preached that preparedness was the best way to dissuade potential enemies from undertaking attacks. But when attacked, he was always an aggressive defensive fighter. In his mind, a passive defense was tantamount to defeat.

MacArthur pointed to the Maginot Line, a vast series of defensive tunnels and forts that France built along its border with Germany in the first half of the 1930s, as a prime example. The Line was originally designed to stop the main German advance with a minimum number of troops, thus enabling France to mount a huge flanking movement with the majority of its armies.

Unfortunately, the French came to see the Line as an adequate defense in and of itself. In 1940, Hitler simply drove his mechanized armies through Belgium and the Netherlands, isolated the Maginot Line, and forced France's surrender. MacArthur explained it as follows:

> *But when the war actually came, the French made the fatal mistake of not carrying out an envelopment maneuver, and remained in passive resistance only. The Maginot Line came to be the universal symbol of static defense, whereas it was meant to be the pivot of a bold offense.*

MacArthur faced the same choice between passive and aggressive defense in the first year of WWII. Although he made the choice for an aggressive defense during the Japanese invasion of the Philippines, choosing to stop the enemy on the beach, he did not have a powerful enough force to successfully carry off the strategy.

In February 1942, while trapped on Corregidor, MacArthur was still advising Army Chief of Staff George C. Marshall to mount an aggressive defense in the Pacific. "The Japanese are sweeping southward in a great offensive and the Allies are attempting merely to stop them by building up forces in the front. This method, as has always been the case in war, will fail." Instead, he stated:

> *Counsels of timidity based upon theories of safety first will not win against such an aggressive and audacious adversary as Japan. No building program no matter of what proportions will be able to overtake the initial advantages the enemy with every chance of success is trying to gain. The only way to beat him is to fight him incessantly.*

A month later, MacArthur landed in Australia. The Australian Chiefs of Staff had considered a defensive plan along the so-called Brisbane Line. In the case of Japanese invasion, a foregone conclusion at that time, the plan called for the abandonment of the west and north of the continent and the creation of a defense line encompassing the industrial and agricultural centers and major ports in the region surrounding Melbourne and Brisbane. MacArthur vehemently disagreed with the plan, saying:

> *The concept was purely one of passive defense, and I felt it would result only in eventual defeat. Even if so restrictive a scheme were tactically successful, its result would be to trap us indefinitely on an island continent ringed by conquered territories and hostile ocean, bereft of all hope of ever assuming the offensive.*

Instead, MacArthur advocated an aggressive defense that moved forward to meet the enemy advance in New Guinea. It proved to be the right strategy. The Allied forces stopped the Japanese in their bid to take Port Moresby, the last defensive stronghold before Australia, later that same year. And MacArthur used that momentum to launch the first successful land offensive of the war at Buna. By January 1943, the tide of the war had turned.

MacArthur demonstrated that it does not matter whether leaders are fighting offensive or defensive actions; their ultimate aim always remains victory. Thus, he declared:

> *It doesn't matter how much you have, so long as you fight with what you have. It doesn't matter where you fight, so long as you fight. Because where you fight, the enemy has to fight, too, and even though it splits your force, it must split his force also. So fight, on whatever the scale, whenever and wherever you can. There is only one way to win victories. Attack, attack, attack!*

This approach to defensive battle led Congressman Ike Skelton to write:

> *MacArthur operationalized the words of Karl von Clausewitz, written 118 years earlier: "A swift and vigorous transition to attack—the flashing sword of vengeance—is the most brilliant point of the defense."*

"The concept was purely one of passive defense, and I felt it would result only in eventual defeat."

Reflection Questions:

- Are you passively or aggressively defending your organization's markets and customers?

- Can you surprise a competitor by transforming a defensive action into an offensive strategy?

Chapter 16

Act Alone When You Must

By definition, leadership encompasses the task of establishing the mission and direction of organizations. A leader's ability to create consensus among stakeholders and build coalitions to achieve the organizational mission are highly desirable supporting factors for this work. But, when the inability to create consensus and coalitions leads to paralysis and blocks an organization from achieving its mission and objectives, it is the leader's responsibility to act unilaterally.

MacArthur acted unilaterally to great effect during the Japanese occupation by blocking Soviet Russia's influence on the governance and restructuring of the defeated nation. Immediately following the surrender, the Russians demanded that they be allowed to occupy the northern Japanese island of Hokkaido. When MacArthur refused, General Kuzma Derevyanko threatened to take the action without U.S. approval. MacArthur later said, "I told him that if a single Soviet soldier entered Japan without my authority, I would at once throw the entire Soviet mission, including himself, into jail." The Russians chose not test his resolve.

Next, a number of nations, hungry for reparations and revenge, demanded a more active role in the occupation of Japan. MacArthur said:

> *As winter approached, the Russians and the British intensified their pressure for a division of the unilateral power being exercised by the United States in the occupation. These two powers insisted that Japan be divided*

> *into spheres of Allied responsibility. It was already evident that the division of Germany into separate zones of occupation had been a serious mistake. I refused to allow it.*

The State Department, in the meantime, was negotiating with the Russians over that nation's aggressive action in the establishment of the Iron Curtain in Eastern Europe. In those negotiations, in return for bargaining leverage in Europe, the Truman Administration was considering the creation of an Allied commission to set policy in Japan. MacArthur first attempted to forestall the process by covertly threatening resignation. One of his staff members was quoted in the media to that effect.

Although the leaked threat appeared to have gained Truman's attention, it did not stop the establishment of two groups of Allied overseers, albeit with limited powers. The Far Eastern Commission was located in Washington and had policy powers. The Allied Council for Japan was an advisory group meant to counsel the Supreme Commander in Tokyo.

Determined to maintain the democratic roots of Japan's transformation, MacArthur froze out the Allied Council. He attended only its first meeting and never allowed it to take a significant role in the business of governing Japan. In 1977, Japanese journalist Isamu Suzkawa said:

> *[W]e are thankful to MacArthur in many ways—in more than one way. One is the fact that it was he who was instrumental in keeping the Russians out of occupied Japan. That, I think, is foremost. If Japan had been under the occupation not only of the American forces but of the Russian, the Chinese, and the British, and so forth, can you imagine what sort of condition Japan would be in now? Look at what's happening in Germany, Korea, or in other places [where] the country is divided into two or three different sections.*

During the Korean War, MacArthur was also firmly convinced that the United States should be acting unilaterally if required. After the Chinese entered the war and the forces of the United Nations were driven back below the 38th Parallel once more, a good deal of pressure, from UN members and particularly from the British, was exerted on Truman to negotiate a cease-fire and prevent any expansion of the conflict. MacArthur, of course, saw no substitute for victory and labeled this "appeasement." After his recall, he renewed his call for unilateral action, declaring:

I have been amazed and deeply concerned, since my return, to observe the extent to which the orientation of our national policy tends to depart from the traditional courage, vision, and forthrightness which has animated and guided our great leaders of the past, to be now largely influenced, if not indeed dictated from abroad and dominated by fear of what others may think or others may do…Never before have we geared national policy to timidity and fear.

In his first day of congressional testimony, on May 3, 1951, MacArthur said:

My hope would be of course that the United Nations would see the wisdom and utility of that course [aggressive defensive action against China], but if they did not, I still believe that the interest of the United States being the predominant one in Korea, would require our action.

"Alone?" inquired Senator Theodore Green. MacArthur replied:

Alone, if necessary. If the other nations of the world haven't got enough sense to see where appeasement leads after the appeasement which led to the Second World War in Europe, if they can't see exactly the road that they are following in Asia, why then we had better protect ourselves and go it alone.

"Alone, if necessary."

Reflection Questions:

- Do you exhaust all cooperative alternatives before taking unilateral action?

- What are your decision-making criteria for undertaking unilateral action?

☆☆☆☆☆

PART THREE

INSPIRATIONAL LEADERSHIP

Chapter 17

Unify Command

The foundational lesson of inspirational leadership is that there must be a clear leader. Committees and management teams are rarely charismatic; they do not easily inspire the energy and loyalty of followers. Further, management-by-committee has some inherent dangers, not the least of which is a lumbering bureaucracy that excels at discussion but impedes speed and flexibility.

MacArthur's father told him, "Doug, councils of war breed timidity and defeatism." The son always heeded the warning and held fast to the principle of unity of command. Whenever possible, MacArthur insisted on a formal chain of command leading to a clearly identified and empowered leader.

In the Pacific Theater during most of WWII, leadership was not unified. After his successful escape to Australia, MacArthur was the ranking officer and was most qualified to assume command in the Pacific, but the Navy refused to give him charge of their fleet. MacArthur, who felt strongly about unity of command, offered to step aside for another leader. He later said:

> *Of all the faulty decisions of the war, perhaps the most unexplainable one was the failure to unify the command in the Pacific. The principle involved is the most fundamental one in the doctrine and tradition of command. In*

> *this instance, it did not involve choosing one individual out of a number of Allied officers, although it was an accepted and entirely successful practice in the other great theaters. The failure to do so in the Pacific cannot be defended in logic, in theory, or in common sense…It resulted in divided effort; the waste, diffusion, and duplication of force; and the consequent extension of the war, with added casualties and cost.*

One reason why MacArthur was so adamant about unity of command was that he had witnessed the confusion and tragedy that can result when military units receive conflicting orders. Near the end of WWI, with the Germans in full retreat, Pershing and his staff were anxious to be the first to enter Sedan. As a result, both I Corps and V Corps were ordered to drive forward through the night, regardless of the previously set boundaries between the allied forces. Interestingly, the usually aggressive MacArthur reacted with caution. He requested and received permission to hold the 84th Brigade back until morning. In the night, several American units crossed their own lines. MacArthur was even briefly captured by an American patrol when investigating the confusion. And when American units encroached on French forces, some were caught in friendly artillery fire.

MacArthur was determined to avoid chaos in command in the Pacific, but it was not to be. Instead, the command was split into two regions. MacArthur was assigned the southwest Pacific region, with its greater land mass; the Navy, under Admiral Chester Nimitz, was given the rest of the Pacific.

The result, as MacArthur predicted, was a great deal of interservice rivalry and competition. Often, both theaters pursued different strategies and competed for resources. In those instances, MacArthur had difficulty getting the ships he needed to island-hop; Nimitz had difficulty getting troops. "The customary petty bickering reached Jovian heights as general was pitted against admiral, or admiral against general in a mighty defense of long and bitterly held prerogatives," said Paul Rogers, who witnessed the infighting from MacArthur's headquarters.

Perhaps the greatest failure of the split command occurred during the return to the Philippines, in the invasion of Leyte. In the famous Battle of Leyte Gulf, the Japanese Navy laid a trap for the American fleet. It used a carrier force as bait and successfully drew the 3rd Fleet, under Navy command, away from Leyte. The Japanese then sent their main naval force to attack the 7th Fleet, under MacArthur's command and still in the gulf, and the land forces on the beach. The only thing that saved the Americans from total destruction was Japanese Admiral Kurita's mistaken decision to break away from the fight. He simply did not realize that he was winning the battle.

MacArthur used the near-disaster at Letye to reiterate the lesson of unity of command. In December 1944, he drafted a message to the War Department, which said, in part:

> *After having narrowly avoided disaster in the Leyte operation as the result of the absence of coordinated naval command, we now enter the more difficult Luzon phase under the same handicap...We shall again enter battle with our naval forces split into two elements under commanders who are thousands of miles apart. The fleets themselves will operate in the same waters against the same enemy, covered by air elements under different commanders...The present arrangement divides the potential of resource, and under guise of unity of command in an artificially compartmented area, makes impossible a unified effort. The situation is thoroughly bad and for a local commander who carries responsibility for results is becoming intolerable.*

"Failure to place undivided responsibility and command in one commander may result in the failure of the operation."

Reflection Questions:

- Do you have the authority to lead?

- Is the chain of command in your organization unimpeded and clearly understood by every employee?

Chapter 18

Be a Role Model

For better or for worse, leaders are the most influential role models within their organizations. Leaders' actions, even more than their words, communicate their values, priorities, and expectations to their followers. Great leaders live up to their words and offer an example that their followers can emulate.

Much of the larger-than-life image that MacArthur created for himself was meant as a model for his officers and troops to follow. He knew that his example as commander set the tone and style of his command. He also knew that it had the power to inspire others.

MacArthur's unfailing optimism was one way in which he acted as a role model. On Corregidor, when MacArthur was besieged by the Japanese and forced to operate from tunnels deep under Malinta Hill, General Carlos Romulo remembered:

> *He always swung into the USAFFE lateral as if bringing great news. Often he would stop at the desk of a staff officer as he went by, offering some comment or advice which, though seldom humorous, was usually optimistic.*

In Australia, when air chief George Kenney reported on the sad state of their air force, MacArthur's response buoyed his spirits. Kenney explained:

Optimism is axiomatic with leadership. And in those grave days and hours, four words from MacArthur meant as much to me as a new squadron of airplanes. Those words were: "George, we'll do it." That attitude breeds victory and success.

As a leader, MacArthur also provided a much-needed model of courage and the will to win. Just days after arriving in Australia in March 1942, he began rallying the spirit of the nation. He stood at a state dinner in the Government House and said:

My faith in our ultimate victory is invincible, and I bring to you tonight the unbreakable spirit of the free man's military code in support of our just cause. That code has come down to us from even before days of knighthood and chivalry. It will stand the test of any ethics or philosophies the world has ever known. It embraces the things that are right and condemns the things that are wrong. Under its banner the free men of the world are united today. There can be no compromise. We shall win or we shall die, and to this end I pledge you the full resources of all the mighty power of my country and all the blood of my countrymen.

Finally, MacArthur used his position as leader to model the policies and changes he wanted to implement. While MacArthur was working to implant democratic values in Japan, many of its citizens thought of him as a living god, much like the Emperor. Crowds would gather outside his building to watch him enter and leave. On one occasion, when a woman prostrated herself before him, he helped her to her feet, saying, "Now, now—we don't do that sort of thing anymore."

MacArthur also made sure to exhibit his support for the Occupation's reforms in women's suffrage. In 1946, when the first women elected to the Japanese Diet were ignored by their male counterparts, MacArthur made his feelings on the issue clear by inviting the new female representatives to his office and giving a speech celebrating their achievements, which was released to the press.

The importance that MacArthur placed on the responsibility of a leader to demonstrate and maintain the highest standard of behavior was clearly evident in his review of the trial of General Masaharu Homma. Homma had led the Japanese invasion of the Philippines. The Bataan Death March, during which 8,000 American and Filipino captives died, had occurred during his command. In the next seven weeks, 28,000 more of the troops died in prison camps under Homma's authority. After the war, Homma was returned to the Philippines, where he was tried by a U.S. military commission and sentenced to death. MacArthur approved the sentence and wrote:

> *The proceedings show the defendant lacked the basic firmness of character and moral fortitude essential to officers charged with the high command of military forces in the field. No nation can safely trust its martial honor to leaders who do not maintain the universal code which distinguishes between those things that are right and those that are wrong.*
>
> *Soldiers of an army invariably reflect the attitude of their General. The leader is the essence. Isolated cases of rapine may well be exceptional, but widespread and continuing abuse can only be the fixed responsibility of highest field authority. Resultant liability is commensurate with resultant crime.*

"Soldiers of an army invariably reflect the attitude of their General."

Reflection Questions:

- Are you aware of how your actions, statements, and behaviors affect others?

- Can the people in your organization and community proudly follow your example?

Chapter 19

Visibility Matters

The presence of a leader enhances the morale and accountability of followers. In good times and particularly, in bad times, leaders must share in the action by taking a prominent place in the midst of their followers. Inspirational leaders are visible leaders.

MacArthur was a firm believer in "being there." He knew the impact that a commander's presence could have on his troops. In early 1942, when MacArthur moved to Corregidor, he first established his headquarters and personal quarters "Topside" (that is, on the highest point of the island). "As an evidence of assurance to these people suffering from deprivation, destruction, and despair," he said, "I deemed it advisable to locate headquarters as prominently as possible, notwithstanding exposure to enemy attack." It was destroyed when regular Japanese bombing raids began soon after.

The headquarters was relocated into the Malinta Tunnel, but MacArthur made a regular practice of leaving the tunnel during air raids. He later explained:

> *There was nothing of bravado in this. It was simply my duty. The gunners at the batteries, the men in the foxholes, they too were in the open. They liked to see me with them at such moments. The subtle corrosion of panic or fatigue, or the feeling of just being fed up, can only be arrested by the intervention of the leader.*

MacArthur was right. Thirty years later, General John Wright, then a first lieutenant, remembered a "terrific barrage" of mortar shells, which destroyed the junior officers' mess, wounding and killing many men, and the resultant panic:

> *But General MacArthur just stood there in the open, giving orders and directing men with great calmness and confidence. He seemed utterly oblivious to fear of the incoming mortar rounds. He was completely unconcerned for his own safety and set an impressive example for us junior officers.*

In 1943, when General Kenney was planning the first major parachute jump of the war at Nadzab in New Guinea, MacArthur insisted on accompanying the troops on the flight to bolster their confidence. When Kenney protested that the risk was too high, he replied, "Honestly, the only thing that disturbs me is the possibility that when we hit the rough air over the mountains my stomach might get upset. I'd hate to get sick and disgrace myself in front of the kids." MacArthur was awarded the Air Medal for his participation on the operation.

Visibility also plays a key role in reinforcing a leader's messages. As superintendent at West Point, he broke precedent by auditing classes and evaluating them with the professors afterward. During the 1928 Olympics, MacArthur not only met regularly with the coaches and players, he took to the field. "When the events were underway, MacArthur seemed to be everywhere at once," wrote biographer D. Clayton James, "he lived the glories and disappointments of the outcomes as intensely as any of the athletes. As the 10,000-meter race was nearing its close finish (won by a Finn), MacArthur was so carried away by the excitement that he rushed from the officials' box to the sideline near the ribbon. On another day, when the University of California's eight-oared shell was rowing to victory on the Sloten River, MacArthur had his chauffeur drive him along the Bank parallel to the shell as it raced."

MacArthur passed the real test of leadership by refusing to hide when visibility might harm his reputation and career. When President Hoover ordered him to undertake the highly unpopular act of evicting the Bonus Army of WWI veterans from Washington in July 1932, his aide Major Dwight D. Eisenhower recommended that MacArthur not be present. MacArthur disagreed. He later said:

The MacArthur family at Ford Selden, NM, circa 1884. His parents taught him the values of patriotism, integrity, and honesty long before he entered school.

Unable to obtain a presidential appointment to West Point, MacArthur earned his appointment with the highest score in Wisconsin Rep. Theabold Otjen's competitive examination in 1898.

MacArthur (#96 in the forefront) gained his lifelong love of learning and athletics at West Texas Military Academy. (Photo circa 1896)

"The Fighting Dude." Brigadier General MacArthur, Commander of the 84th Brigade of the Rainbow Division, in Croix Valanche, France, 1918.

MacArthur hosting the Prince of Wales at West Point. As superintendent (1919–1922), he sought to expand the cadets' exposure to new ideas and current events.

President of the American Olympic Committee, MacArthur shepherded the U.S. team to its first place finish in the Ninth Olympiad, Amsterdam, 1928.

Army Chief of Staff MacArthur receives the Legion of Honor from France's Minister of Defense Andre Maginot, 1931. Less than a decade later, the Maginot Line became a potent symbol of the danger of a passive defense.

MacArthur and Philippines President Quezon, July 1941. At age 61, after most of his contemporaries had already retired, MacArthur was recalled to active duty as Commanding General, U.S. Army Forces in the Far East.

On September 5, 1943, MacArthur flew with the troops to Nadzab to bolster their confidence before the first major parachute jump in the Southwest Pacific.

MacArthur on the beach at Los Negros just hours after the invasion was launched, February 29, 1944. Satisfied that the position could be held, he ordered the completion of the reconnaissance in force.

MacArthur called on the people of the Philippines to "rise and strike" from the beach at Leyte on the day of his return, October 20, 1944.

MacArthur with the troops on Morotai, September 15, 1944. By “hitting ’em where they ain’t,” he established a base of operations within 300 miles of the Philippines at the cost of only 31 American lives.

During the drive to recapture Manila (circa January 1945), MacArthur took to the road to goad his generals into moving faster.

Winston Churchill called MacArthur's arrival at Atsugi Airport in Japan on August 30, 1945, the greatest "of all the amazing acts of bravery of the war."

MacArthur returns to Corregidor almost three years to the day after being forced to leave to escape capture by the Japanese, March 2, 1945.

Aboard the USS Missouri, September 2, 1945. MacArthur signs the Japanese surrender flanked by Generals Wainwright and Percival, who had been imprisoned as POWs since 1942.

MacArthur and Hirohito, September 27, 1945. MacArthur's nonchalant demeanor and informality effectively communicated his authority over the Emperor and sent an unmistakable message to the people of Japan.

MacArthur conceived the Inchon assault as he watched the North Korean People's Army overrun Seoul on June 29, 1950, just days into the war.

MacArthur and President Harry Truman at their only meeting, Wake Island, October 15, 1950.

Japanese line the route to the airport in a show of respect as MacArthur obeys Truman's recall order, April 16, 1951.

MacArthur returns to the U.S. mainland after a 14-year absence. Over 500,000 San Franciscans welcomed him home, April 17, 1951.

Old soldiers may never die, but MacArthur did not intend to fade away. Over 20 million Americans watched him address Congress in an historic television broadcast, April 19, 1951.

MacArthur with John F. Kennedy in the White House, July 1961. He advised President Kennedy and later, President Johnson, to avoid war in Vietnam.

> *I accompanied the troops in person, anticipating the possibility of such a serious situation arising that necessary decisions might lie beyond the purview of responsibility of any subordinate commander, and with the purpose of obtaining a personal familiarity with every phase of the troops' activities.*

In WWII, when troop and shipping shortages forced the cancellation of the rotation policy designed to return soldiers to the United States after fixed periods of combat, MacArthur took the added steps of writing and personally signing each copy of the order, which was posted at the same time in each of the units under his command. Colonel Aubrey Newman later said:

> *[The troops] realized he knew what such a reversal of policy meant to them, and he showed his confidence in them as military men that they would understand that this was the proper course to follow, hard as it might be. No one had ever before seen Gen. MacArthur's personal signature, much less on an order that, in effect, bypassed every echelon of command to go from him to the individual men in the ranks, explaining directly to them why the decision was made, and that he had made it... As a result there was no loss of morale, only soldierly acceptance of a fact of war.*

"Leadership is often crystallized in some sort of public gesture."

Reflection Questions:

- Do you practice what Tom Peters and the founders of Hewlett-Packard dubbed MBWA (Management By Walking Around)?

- When times are tough are you and your organization's managers leading from the front?

Chapter 20

Cultivate Image

Leaders, by definition, play an iconic role within and as representatives of their organizations. Leaders' images are not an exact reflection of who they are; rather, they are a reflection of how leaders are perceived by others. Charismatic leaders almost invariably cultivate and manage that reflection.

MacArthur was an expert at image management. His public appearance—dress, speech, and physical manner—all reflected a cultivated image, a near-perfect representation of natural authority. Britain's Lord Mountbatten, who commanded the Southeast Asia Theater in WWII, was struck by MacArthur's ability to assume his public persona. He said:

> *[MacArthur] does not look at all fierce or commanding until he puts his famous embroidered cap on. As we went out together to face the photographers and he pulled his cap on, his whole manner changed. His jaw stuck out and he looked aggressive and tough, but as soon as the photographers had finished, he relaxed completely, took off his hat, and was his old charming self.*

MacArthur was also enamored with props, possibly because they made him instantly recognizable. In WWI and at West Point, his riding crop was always in evidence. Later, he adjusted his image and carried a cane, which was more of a prop than a necessity. It lasted for several decades, until in WWII, Colonel Sid Huff returned from a trip to the United States and told MacArthur, "One of the things people asked me was this: 'Why does MacArthur cart that cane around all the time? Is he feeble?'" The cane was never seen again. His corncob pipes and aviator sunglasses were his most famous accessories, and they became popular with the general public because he used them.

In WWII and after, MacArthur's props also served to draw attention away from tremors in his hands, a condition that was noted by many who had personal contact with him. So, his accessories helped preserve the youthful and vigorous image of a man who had undertaken huge command responsibilities well past the standard retirement age.

MacArthur's uniform and accessories were, in a very real sense, designed to convey a desired message. Marine General Edwin Simmons described him coming ashore at Inchon in September 1950 like this:

> *MacArthur was in full costume, the crushed hat, the sunglasses, the leather jacket, the faded but carefully pressed khaki trousers that you know the curious thing is that he, General MacArthur, so dominated that scene although there were many other notables and dignitaries in the party…He completely dominated the scene.*

In the Philippines, where the citizens responded to pomp, MacArthur created an imposing uniform that corresponded with his position as Field Marshal. According to biographer D. Clayton James, it was white sharkskin with black trousers and fully adorned with braid and brass. During WWII, when fighting a war was the business of the day, he eschewed glitz for the simple look of a soldier. He wore a khaki working uniform consisting of an open-necked shirt and trousers. He wore a worn officer's hat with scrambled egg braid. He did not wear any of his decorations, just the insignia of rank on both sides of the collar. This was also the uniform MacArthur wore at the Japanese surrender aboard the *U.S.S. Missouri.*

Taken to extremes, the details of image can appear foolish, but there is an undeniable power there. To see the power of image at work, examine what has become the most famous photograph of the Japanese Occupation (in the photo section): the image of MacArthur and Emperor Hirohito, taken on the occasion of their first meeting.

In fact, the entire meeting was a highly effective exercise in image building. MacArthur demonstrated his authority by *not* calling on the

Emperor after arriving in Japan. Instead, he waited for Hirohito to request an audience and travel to MacArthur's office, an unprecedented break with that nation's protocol.

MacArthur did not change his appearance for the meeting. He met Hirohito in his usual plain khaki uniform—no jacket, no decorations, or hat; only the five-star insignia of rank. Before the meeting, the two men posed together for a photo. MacArthur stands relaxed with hands in back pockets; a dominant, highlighted figure in light attire who is more than a head taller than Hirohito, who is rigid as if at attention in dark formal attire with shoulders sloped downward and his hands at his sides.

The message in the image, which was released to the press and reprinted throughout Japan, was abundantly clear. "This single picture," said Japanese historian and author Rinjiro Sodei, "certainly changed the Japanese mentality. Everyone knew who is the ruler of Japan and this is it."

The conversation between MacArthur and Hirohito was immaterial compared to the circumstances under which the meeting took place and the resulting photograph. In this case, as Marshall McLuhan said, the medium was the message.

"I studied dramatics for seven years under General MacArthur."—Attributed to Dwight D. Eisenhower

Reflection Questions:

- Does your appearance and bearing help or hinder the image you are trying to create?

- What is the first impression given to visitors to your organization?

Chapter 21

Make Compelling Speeches

Public speaking scares people. In fact, *The Book of Lists* ranks fear of speechmaking as our number one fear, above the fear of death. It is, nevertheless, a fear that leaders cannot afford to indulge. Leaders must be compelling orators who are capable of engaging intimately with groups and convincing those groups to act as needed.

MacArthur is remembered as one of history's great speechmakers. His public speaking has been accurately characterized as "grandiloquent," a word that connotes a bombastic style of speechmaking that seems less relevant today than a century ago. At the same time, however, MacArthur was an extraordinarily effective speaker. Along with Roosevelt and Churchill, his words continue to highlight the milestones of the mid-20th century.

After President Truman recalled him from Korea in 1951, approximately 20 million Americans watched MacArthur deliver his famous "Old Soldiers" speech before Congress. MacArthur's performance stood in stark contrast to Truman's plain-spoken and less-than-focused speech that announced the recall. D. Clayton James described it like this:

> *After standing silently before the battery of microphones for nearly three minutes while the audience stood and applauded again, [MacArthur] began the thirty-seven-minute address that would be ranked later as one of the most impressive and divisive oratorial performances of recent American times. He spoke in an unhurried, yet incredibly forceful manner, his voice sounding deeply resonant and his phrases and sentences blending eloquence*

and sincerity, emotionalism and sweeping generalizations, in a way that moved even many listeners who found his logic and his proposals faulty or downright dangerous.

In the speech, MacArthur described his strategy for winning the Korean War and made his case against limited war and the course of "appeasement" he believed the Truman administration had undertaken. But he did more than that; he connected to his audiences on an emotional level.

In the closing paragraphs of his speech, he pled for the Koreans and the U.S. troops who were paying the ultimate price for the war. And he closed with a richly sentimental portrayal of himself as one of the "old soldiers who never die" but simply fade away. Out of context, it sounds maudlin and silly. In the Capitol Building, Congressmen and spectators wept. Afterward, Speaker of the House Joe Martin, who had given the press the letter from MacArthur that became the final straw for Truman, told reporters, "Well, boys, there's only one thing I can say: there wasn't a dry eye on the Republican side, and there wasn't a dry seat on the Democratic side."

MacArthur's greatest skill as an orator was this ability to connect to his intended audience. One way in which he accomplished this was by putting himself into his speeches, by personalizing the appeal. The best of many examples is in the "Rally to me" speech, broadcast from the beach during the invasion at Leyte to the people of the Philippines. MacArthur said:

I have returned. By the grace of Almighty God our forces stand again on Philippine soil—soil consecrated in the blood of our two peoples. We have come, dedicated and committed, to the task of destroying every vestige of enemy control over your daily lives, and of restoring, upon a foundation of indestructible strength, the liberties of your people.

At my side is your President, Sergio Osmena, worthy successor of that great patriot, Manuel Quezon, with members of his cabinet. The seat of your government is now therefore firmly re-established on Philippine soil.

The hour of your redemption is here. Your patriots have demonstrated an unswerving and resolute devotion to the principles of freedom that challenges the best that is written on the pages of human history. I now call upon your supreme effort that the enemy may know from the temper of an aroused and outraged people within that he has a force there to contend with no less violent than is the force committed without.

> *Rally to me! Let the indomitable spirit of Bataan and Corregidor lead on. As the lines of battle roll forward to bring you within the zones of operation, rise and strike! For your homes and hearths, strike! For future generations of your sons and daughters, strike! In the name of your sacred dead, strike! Let no heart be faint. Let every arm be steeled. The guidance of Divine God points the way. Follow in His name to the Holy Grail of righteous victory.*

In this speech, MacArthur declared his promise to the Filipinos fulfilled and, with the authority and power that act conferred upon him, called them to arms. He also struck a strong psychological blow against the enemy. The Japanese had been plagued by Filipino and American guerillas. There were an estimated 180,000 guerilla fighters on the islands, and now this phantom army was being ordered to emerge and attack.

MacArthur also utilized repetition to drive his words home. "Strike!" he said, over and over. It is the final word in four sentences in the speech's final paragraph, emphasized each time.

Finally, those who study MacArthur's oration note his delivery. "He sometimes delivered public addresses of more than an hour in length without any notes whatsoever," said President Eisenhower. "However, he was not speaking extemporaneously. He always learned by rote his speeches." Because MacArthur memorized his speeches, he was able to devote greater attention to his gestures and vocal patterns instead of unadorned recitation.

"This is the Voice of Freedom,
General MacArthur speaking."

Reflection Questions:

- How can you make your speeches appear extemporaneous?

- Are you putting yourself into your speeches and making a personal connection with your audience?

Chapter 22

Demand Results When Necessary

Leadership is not a popularity contest. Leaders are accountable for organizational results, and they are responsible for imposing accountability on their followers. Often, this accountability is a routine part of organizational life. But there are also times when desired outcomes are critical and/or not forthcoming. Then, a leader must be willing and able to demand both sacrifices and results.

MacArthur knew from personal experience that there were times when a commander was forced to demand results, no matter the cost. During the summer of 1918, MacArthur and the Rainbow Division were on the receiving end of one such order. The division had been attached to the French Fourth Army and assigned to stop a major German offensive when this message came from General Henri Gouraud, "The bombardment will be terrible. You will stand it without weakness...None shall look to the rear; none shall yield a step. Each shall have but one thought: to kill, to kill, until they have had their fill. Therefore your General says to you: You will break this assault and it will be a happy day." Gouraud's demand was fulfilled. The German offensive was stopped, and the tide of the war turned.

Later that same year, in the Meuse-Argonne Offensive, MacArthur's brigade was assigned to take the German stronghold at Côte de Châtillon. MacArthur studied the target and told his divisional commander that he was unsure whether they could capture it. The night before the attack,

General Charles Summerall, the corps commander, entered MacArthur's command post. "Give me Châtillon, or a list of five thousand casualties," he demanded. A startled MacArthur replied, "All right, General, we'll take it or my name will head the list." The bitter fight took three days, but Châtillon was taken.

MacArthur himself preferred to give his orders in the form of a request. But he did not hesitate to step in and demand results when necessary. In December 1942, when the commanding general in the field could not win the prolonged and difficult battle for Buna in Papua, MacArthur summoned General Robert Eichelberger to his headquarters. He told Eichelberger:

> *Bob, I'm putting you in command at Buna. Relieve Harding. I am sending you in, Bob, and I want you to remove all officers who won't fight. Relieve Regimental and Battalion commanders; if necessary put Sergeants in charge of Battalions and Corporals in charge of companies—anyone who will fight. Time is of the essence; the Japs may land reinforcements any night...I want you to take Buna, or not come back alive.*

In the next month, Eichelberger engineered one of the notable turnarounds of the war. He took command in the field, and revitalized and reorganized his command. More importantly, he also received the tanks and heavy artillery needed to break through the enemy's defensive lines. Buna fell on January 2, 1943, and the first major Army victory against the Japanese was won.

MacArthur's approach to peacetime endeavors followed a similar pattern. His policy during the Japanese Occupation was to try to institute change through the preestablished authority of the Japanese government. However, when the government was not responsive on issues that he considered essential, MacArthur demanded and got action.

In late 1945, MacArthur asked the Japanese politicians to draft a new, more democratic constitution. Predictably, the Japanese created a commission to study the issue but did not rush into process. MacArthur began to get impatient. In February 1946, after a draft of a revised constitution created by the committee (which showed few significant changes) was leaked to the Japanese press, his impatience turned into action.

MacArthur ordered the SCAP Government Section to produce a constitution for the Japanese. "The next month—from February 4 to March 6, when the draft of the new constitution was made public—was one of the most extraordinary periods of the occupation," wrote Richard Finn, who served as a U.S. Foreign Service officer in Japan. "The U.S. military command wrote a basic national constitution for the defeated nation in utmost secrecy and then made sure it was approved by Japan's political leaders with only a few changes."

The new constitution was prepared in just seven days. MacArthur, who took an active hand in creating the draft, approved it on February 12. The next day, Head of GS General Whitney and his staff presented it to Japanese Prime Minister Yoshida and the head of the constitution reform committee. The Japanese were informed that they must adopt it and, after several ineffectual attempts to modify it, finally did on March 5. MacArthur's press release said, "It is with a sense of deep satisfaction that I am today able to announce the decision of the Emperor and government of Japan to submit to the Japanese people a new and enlightened constitution which has my full approval."

"I want you to take Buna, or not come back alive."

Reflection Questions:

- Do you give ultimatums sparingly and only when necessary?

- How do your followers know which organizational results are critical?

Chapter 23

Expect the Best

Psychologists call it a *self-fulfilling prophecy*: Physicians know it as the *placebo effect*. Whatever you call it, it is a proven fact: people tend to get the results that they expect. This is why inspirational leaders can bolster the confidence and performance of their followers simply by believing in them. By communicating that belief to their followers, leaders often get exactly the results they expect.

There is no doubt that MacArthur was a believer in this phenomenon. General John J. Pershing related the following incident that had taken place before a battle in WWI:

> *[MacArthur] went forward to the battalion that was to lead the way. He said to the Major in command, "Now, when the barrage lifts, I want you to go forward with your men and lead the way. Don't stand back. They will follow you. You can't take it by standing back and telling them to go ahead, but you show the way and you can take it—right up to the top. You do this and I will see that you get the Distinguished Service Cross."*
>
> *Then MacArthur stepped back and looked at him and said, "I see you are going to do it. You've got it now," took his own Distinguished Service Cross decoration, pinned it on him as the barrage lifted. It was one of the greatest cases of intelligence, psychological leadership and direction I have ever encountered.*

MacArthur's expectations bolstered the confidence of his subordinates. In 1936, when MacArthur was creating the Philippines military, Sid Huff accepted the job of naval advisor. In his first meeting on the job, MacArthur told Huff that he wanted a fleet of motor torpedo boats, forerunners of the PT boat, and asked how many Huff could deliver in ten years. When Huff replied that he had never even seen a torpedo boat, MacArthur told him, "That's all right. You will…You're a Navy man and you know what to do."

In the memoirs of his years with MacArthur, Huff wrote, "I began to think I could do it, perhaps because it was MacArthur who told me to do it. I had a feeling, too, that he would not interfere and, if I did a good job, he would back me up to the end. In time, that feeling was confirmed."

MacArthur's expectation of followers also became a motivation in and of itself. William Ganoe, MacArthur's chief of staff at West Point, explained:

> *[MacArthur] made you a driving force with the fewest words of concentrated inspiration. He stretched your talents to the elastic limits. He did not hold back, hedge or give you the slightest hint of uncertainty. There was no cautioning, "Now I'd look out for this," or "If this should happen, try this." There was no nervousness, anticipation of a situation, or implied reservation that he really ought to be handling the matter himself. There was just the plain what, without any hows, whys, ifs, or maybes. You were freed of any cluttering side issues.*
>
> *To a subordinate who had served under commanders who loaded him down with details, cautions, hesitancies, hamperings, and meddlings, it was an emancipation and delight to serve under MacArthur. For him there seemed to be no fear that his agent might not be up to par and no temptation to arrogate everything to himself. He would send his athletics representative away with full powers to make contracts with universities, and his Quartermaster to deal with architects in projects involving millions.*

His subordinates also interpreted MacArthur's expectations and confidence as a sign of his admiration and respect. They became an emotional bond. MacArthur's WWII air chief George Kenney said, "One thing that helped, however, was that a very important guy named Douglas MacArthur believed in me. He would not let me down and I would not let him down. I was quite sure that he knew that, too." Kenney treasured this public affirmation of MacArthur's trust in him:

I got quite a kick that day out of a report of a MacArthur press conference. Some of the newspaper crowd told me about it. The General had finished his talk, when one of the correspondents said, "General, what is the Air Force doing today?" General MacArthur said, "Oh, I don't know. Go ask General Kenney." The newspaperman said, "General, do you mean to say you don't know where the bombs are falling?" MacArthur turned to him, grinned, and said, "Of course, I know where they are falling. They are falling in the right place. Go ask George Kenney where it is."

That was the best compliment I've ever received.

Finally, MacArthur's expectations also acted as a performance bond. Kenney explained, "MacArthur leads—he does not drive. People who work for him drive themselves to carry out his wishes. They feel that they must not let 'the Old Man' down."

"You're the man who can do it."

Reflection Questions:

- Do you expect the best of your followers?

- Do your expectations inspire confidence in your followers, or do they inspire fear and hesitancy?

Chapter 24

Extend the Personal Touch

Leadership eventually comes down to the individual level. A leader makes a connection to an individual follower, and the quality of that connection either reinforces the relationship or undermines it. Inspirational leaders are expert at using the personal touch to establish and maintain positive relationships.

MacArthur, who was often mistakenly criticized for his remoteness, had the personal touch. "Well, I think he had a little bit of what Franklin D. Roosevelt had: this ability to make you feel that you were doing something for him especially," says Frank Rizzo, who worked in the Government Section at SCAP headquarters. Rizzo explained:

> *Let's say it was the top man's ability to engage you with the feeling that it was a privilege to do this for him, that he knew that personally, and that he had asked you personally to do this, whatever it was.*
>
> *For example, when I would meet him someplace he would say, "Thank you very much for taking care of so-and-so." Somebody would come in from Manila, and I would take him around and see that he got his briefings and the rest of it. MacArthur would know about it, and he would thank me personally. He would say, "Frank," he wouldn't say "Mr. Rizzo."*
>
> *Well, after all, this thing that he's talking about is something that I would do anyway. It's part of the business of the section. But he takes it as a personal favor to him and lets me understand that he appreciates it that way. I would say that is a characteristic of a leader. Wouldn't you say so?*

Former Secretary of Defense Caspar Weinberger, who served in MacArthur's Brisbane headquarters as an intelligence officer in WWII, found MacArthur imposing, but not remote. A captain at the time, Weinberger was far from the center of power, but he did meet MacArthur twice.

In one instance, which Weinberger relates in his autobiography, *In the Arena*, he stood aside as MacArthur entered an elevator. MacArthur noticed him waiting and "said, in those deliberate, sonorous, organ-like tones, 'Come, ride along with me, Captain.'"

The second time Weinberger had contact with MacArthur was when a potentially important piece of intelligence arrived the night before an invasion. He delivered it to MacArthur, who (looking as impeccable in his bathrobe as his uniform) read it and said, "Well, what do *you* think, Captain? What would you do?" When Weinberger replied that he thought the operation was not endangered, MacArthur replied, "That's what I think, too."

As Secretary of Defense for President Reagan, Weinberger placed a bust of MacArthur in his office for inspiration. He was also instrumental in the 1981 establishment of the Douglas MacArthur Corridor at the Department of Defense. Today, Weinberger says, "In the few times I saw him, [MacArthur] was perfectly congenial, cordial and friendly."

Although MacArthur was not known for his sense of humor, he would employ it to create a personal connection. On Corregidor, after his Topside living quarters were bombed, Sid Huff helped scavenge furnishings for MacArthur's new quarters. He recalled:

> *Col. Howard Smith and I had to scrounge all over the island and through the Topside rubble to find the things they needed, from an armchair to a refrigerator with a machine-gun-bullet hole through it. We got to be pretty good scroungers and the house was fairly well furnished in a few days. The General didn't directly say anything to me after he saw what we had collected. But when I met him in the tunnel, he quickly side-stepped away from me and put both hands over his pockets and backed up against the wall as if he were afraid I was going to take something away from him.*
>
> *"Go on—go on," he said grinning. "Nothing here to scrounge."*

MacArthur was well aware that the power of the personal touch extended beyond his relationships with subordinates. He also used it to influence and win over his peers and superiors. As Superintendent of West Point, he gave William Ganoe a thorough education in the art of creating personal connections during the periodic visits of the Congressional delegation known as The Board of Visitors. MacArthur told Ganoe:

> *Chief, as far as I can ascertain, this visit has heretofore been looked upon both by visited and visitors as a chore, something they had to go through with, and of doubtful accomplishment. As long as these Congressmen were looked upon as a unit like a squad of soldiers, taken here and there by minions of the Supe, regardless of their likes and dislikes, that sort of result was bound to take place. This time we're not going to do that. These lawmakers deserve their individuality as much as the Prince of Wales. There should exist here on this Post officers from many states. Consult the Congressional Directory. Find out from what states and districts the Congressmen come. Find the most personable officers from those states and districts and attach one appropriately to each Congressman as his official Aide while here.*

"Come, ride along with me, Captain."

Reflection Questions:

- Do you create opportunities to establish personal connections with your followers?

- Do your followers find you approachable and easy to talk to?

☆☆☆☆☆

PART FOUR

MANAGEMENT À LA MACARTHUR

Chapter 25

Principles of Occupation

The management of occupations is one of the most difficult of all leadership tasks. Political and military leaders face the greatest challenges—the occupation of foreign nations and territories. Business and other leaders undertake occupations in the form of mergers and acquisitions. It is a measure of the challenges inherent in the occupations of both nations and organizations that most are deemed failures.

When MacArthur was appointed to lead Japan's occupation, he was well aware of the difficulties. "[H]istory clearly showed," he said, "that no modern military occupation of a conquered nation had been a success." In his eyes, their weakness included:

> *[T]he substitution of civil by military authority; the loss of self-respect and self-confidence by the people; the constantly growing ascendancy of centralized dictatorial power instead of a localized representative system; the lowering of the spiritual and moral tone of a population controlled by foreign bayonets; the inevitable deterioration in the occupying forces themselves as the disease of power infiltrated their ranks.*

MacArthur successfully avoided the worst effects of these traps and, with the help of events, led a highly successful occupation. In sharp contrast to Germany, which was split and remained so for 45 years, Japan remained unified and was again independent by 1952. Twenty-five years later, Japan also boasted one of the world's leading economies.

Here are five principles of management derived from MacArthur's tenure as Japan's proconsul:

1. Empathize and Connect with the People

Although MacArthur knew that the Japanese people must accept responsibility for the war, he neither excessively blamed them nor did he seek to punish them for their leaders' actions. Instead, he quickly communicated his intention to alleviate their sufferings and add to their freedoms. He established himself as a benevolent yet authoritative leader.

MacArthur enlisted the entire occupation army in his quest to "win the hearts and minds" of the Japanese. He refused a War Department missive to restrict fraternization and encouraged the American soldiers to meet and mingle with the people of Japan. "They are our ambassadors," said MacArthur of the troops. "They are our true ambassadors."

2. Create Change Through Established Local Authority

MacArthur has been criticized for his retention and support of Japan's Emperor Hirohito, but this strategy was instrumental in enabling a successful occupation. In Japan, the Emperor was the highest and most revered authority figure. By trading the Emperor's security for his cooperation, MacArthur ensured the acquiescence of the people. He also used the Emperor as a role model on which to build his own image of authority.

Further, although MacArthur certainly initiated most of the fundamental change in Japan, he tried to remain behind the scenes. "I knew that the whole occupation would fail if we did not proceed from this one basic assumption—the reform had to come from the Japanese." By enlisting the Japanese government itself in the creation and endorsement of new legislation and policies, he increased the likelihood of acceptance of radical change by the people.

3. Restore and Keep Order

MacArthur was fortunate in that there was no active violent resistance to the occupation, but he knew that order must be restored and maintained for change to succeed. It was for this reason that his first priorities in Japan were to disarm the nation and feed its people. His "send-me-bread-or-send-me-bullets" message was not written lightly.

Although he preferred not to make public demands, MacArthur did step in and exert his authority to keep order. MacArthur supported labor unions, nevertheless when three million workers threatened a general strike in 1947, he forbid it and threatened force. He supported a free press but closed down a Communist newspaper. Public order was his priority.

4. Enlist Expert Assistance

Occupations often require skills that are outside a leader's competence. "My professional military knowledge was no longer a major factor," explained MacArthur. "I had to be an economist, a political scientist, an engineer, a manufacturing executive, a teacher, even a theologian of sorts."

MacArthur dealt with the need for this wide-ranging expertise by enlisting outside experts to study the major issues of the occupation and recommend strategies to resolve them. He invited civilian experts to work in his headquarters. He also requested specialized expert commissions from the United States.

5. End the Occupation as Soon as Possible

History taught MacArthur that the longer an occupation extended, the greater the odds of failure. In fact, he believed that occupations should last no longer than three years. Accordingly, in 1947—less than two years after the surrender—he began calling for a peace treaty and Japan's full and independent return to the community of nations. "There should be no bayonet control of Nippon once the peace terms have been arranged," he said.

MacArthur maintained that the conditions for ending the occupation had been set at its beginning: They encompassed military, political, and economic goals. In 1947, he stated that the military goals had been met and that the political goals, which would take years to fully establish, had taken root. The final goal of economic stability, he said, would be accomplished when Japan's sovereignty was re-established and the nation was "allowed to trade with the world."

"If any occupation lasts too long, or is not carefully watched from the start, one party becomes slaves and the other masters."

Reflection Questions:

When taking command of existing organizations, ask yourself the following questions:

- What are the major operative elements of the organization's culture and heritage?

- What goals can be more effectively achieved if directed by already established leaders?

Chapter 26

Weigh Change Carefully

Change is an organizational imperative, but the choice of when—and when not—to change is a fundamental leadership issue. Some leaders mistakenly adopt change for its own sake; they create an organizational fetish out of the supposed benefits of constant change. The result: Buffeted by a never-ending stream of new fads and programs-of-the-month, their organizations' priorities become blurred and lapse into chaos. This is why change should never be undertaken without careful analysis.

MacArthur's leadership career was one characterized by many challenging change efforts, yet he always tempered the impetus to change with a practical understanding of the difficulties it entailed. In 1920, for instance, as he took command of West Point, he knew that major changes in its educational programs would be necessary to transform cadets into properly prepared officers.

MacArthur built a case for the benefits of change. He pointed to the growing need for huge armies of citizen-soldiers in wartime. "The type of West Pointer we have been developing," he said, "is not the type suited for the training and leadership of civilians. We need not lower our level, but we must accommodate ourselves to a radical change in the world."

He also identified the potential cost of the changes undertaken at West Point:

> *In meeting this problem, those who were charged with the solution undertook the task with a full realization of its seriousness. It is well understood that it is no light affair to attempt to modify a status which had proved itself so splendidly for a century or more. It is understood that change under the guise of reconstruction was destructive unless clearly and beyond question it introduced something of added benefit.*

MacArthur had no intention of losing the already long-established values and traditions of the Academy or of creating more internal upheaval than necessary. "It was recognized," he further explained, "that reform to be effective must be evolutionary and not revolutionary." To minimize the risk of change, he approached the task in incremental steps.

Understanding that change does not take hold instantaneously, MacArthur also preached the necessity of shepherding and nurturing change programs until they were established. "A program, however, is in itself a lifeless thing, a mere skeleton," he said, "and it has been the constant effort of my administration to put flesh and blood upon it and to imbue it with life."

Deciding whether a change is useful and viable can be difficult. MacArthur himself made the wrong decision on one notable occasion. For all the organizational efficiencies he implemented as Army Chief of Staff, he opposed and helped defeat several bills calling for the creation of a national department of defense, which would have overseen the Army and Navy, and established an independent Air Force. The efficiencies and economies of a united military establishment would not be fully realized until the late 1940s. In 1947, the position of Secretary of Defense was established, as was a separate Air Force. In 1949, the Department of Defense was finally established.

MacArthur realized his error several years before that. In 1942, he was present while General Kenney argued for just such an organizational structure with chief of staff Sutherland. "Much to my surprise," Kenney remembered, "General MacArthur broke into the conversation and said that a single department was the proper organization and that the Air should be separated and have the same autonomy as the land and sea forces." When Kenney reminded MacArthur that he had not believed that in 1932,

MacArthur replied, "No, I didn't. At that time I opposed it with every resource at my command. It was the greatest mistake of my career."

As the turbulent 1960s dawned, MacArthur offered a final warning about change—one that continues to be relevant today. He said:

> *I realize full well that the reckless spirit of the times seeks change. But change should not be made for the sake of change alone. It should be sought only to adapt time-tested principles which have been proven in the crucible of human experience to the new requirements of an expanding society.*

MacArthur was talking about the principles on which America is based. He continued:

> *The Constitution is not to be treated as an instrument of political expediency. Every move that is made to circumvent its spirit, every move that is made to over-centralize political power, every move that is made to curtail and suppress individual liberty is reaction in its most extreme form.*

"...change should not be made for the sake of change alone."

Reflection Questions:

- Do you fully understand the cost of the change before you undertake it?

- How do the pressures of change manifest themselves within your organization?

Chapter 27

Structure for Results

Organizational structure can help or hinder a leader. When form follows function, organizational performance can be maximized. But structural form can also create barriers to the effective functioning of organizations. One manifestation of this is the "Silo Effect," which results when entrenched specialized bureaucracies pursue their own needs without regard to the large needs of the organization they exist to serve.

MacArthur's ability as an administrator of large organizations was widely noted. Dwight Eisenhower said that the skills he gained while working for MacArthur prepared him for his command in Europe in WWII. Aside from advanced study in engineering, however, MacArthur never attended the Army's staff and services schools and colleges, and had no formal education in organizational design. His views on the structure of organizations were developed on the job.

With the creation of SCAP in Japan in 1945, MacArthur created a unique quasi-government that at its peak would grow to 5,000 military and civilian personnel. A notable element in his design was a set of "Special Staff Sections." These units were aligned to the various U.S. goals for the occupation and were assigned responsibility for achieving them. They ensured that SCAP's form would follow and support its function and its ultimate aims.

There are echoes of MacArthur's design for his headquarters in Japan in the "four-army organization" that he designed and implemented while Chief of Staff in the 1930s. When he took the job, the Army was divided into nine corps commands, which were organized around administrative goals and operated autonomously. In case of war, however, MacArthur explained, "there was no complete chain of tactical control…Immediate and unified employment of all units available would be impossible."

To solve the problem, MacArthur oversaw the creation of four armies. These armies were located in four broad areas that encompassed the nine corps commands and covered the northeast and mid-Atlantic states, the Great Lakes region, the southern and southwestern states, and the western states and coast. More importantly, a tactical command structure was established, along with a continuous chain of command that reached to the President. The result, said MacArthur, was that the Department of War could respond to an emergency "as an integrated machine rather than [be] compelled to operate in the confusion of uncoordinated and ineffective action until the necessary staffs and headquarters could be improvised." Again, he ensured that form would follow the highest function of the organization.

MacArthur's organizational designs showed a constant concern for the need for unified command, organizational responsiveness, and the unimpeded flow of information. Also, while Chief of Staff, he revamped the General Staff, which had been organized into five dedicated divisions after WWI. MacArthur found that the borders between the divisions were hardening into walls. There was, he said, "little or no proper meeting of the minds on important subjects. Uncoordinated action has too often resulted. Here and there, administrative work has been taken over by these divisions in violation of the law and to the embarrassment of work of first importance."

To remedy the problem, MacArthur created a general council. This advisory council included the heads of divisions as well as other ranking organizational leaders and regularly met "for the purposes of reviewing and properly coordinating all major War Department projects."

In Australia in WWII, MacArthur was given command of army, navy, and air forces—as well as the Australian military forces. Some of them, the

Army and Navy in particular, had long histories of rivalry. He again sought to create open communication and unified effort through the structure of his command. Headquarters staffer Paul Rogers explained:

> *MacArthur conceived of the entire top structure of the command as a single unit. To counteract a natural tendency on the part of each service to split away, he brought them together in a single location, at least the air and navy commands that were headed by the Americans, who could not easily escape. Blamey occupied separate quarters, on the grounds that he was not only commander of Allied Land Forces but also the ranking officer in the Australian Army. The others were crowded cheek by jowl into 401 Collins Street in Melbourne and later in the AMP Building in Brisbane. They were not always comfortable and happy in their communion, but they were readily accessible to MacArthur, to Sutherland, and to each other.*

General Blamey himself wrote:

> *One of the great advantages of having General Headquarters and the headquarters of the Allied Land Forces, Allied Naval Forces, and Allied Air Forces in close proximity is the immediate interchange of information…all pertinent messages are made available to Land, Naval, and Air Forces regardless of the sources from which the messages are derived. Each operational staff is thus enabled to analyze and interpret the messages with obvious advantage.*

"Effective tactical deployment of an army is wholly impossible in the absence of a complete and properly devised network of command and staff..."

Reflection Questions:

- Do you encourage cooperation and communication among your staff?

- How can the structure of your organization be renovated to better reflect its long-term goals?

Chapter 28

Plan Honestly

Leaders are planners. To achieve more than a random chance of success, they must plan before they act. To maximize their chances of success, they must create and develop plans that are attainable.

MacArthur was a bold and ambitious planner, whose plans were almost always successfully executed because they were realistic in their assumptions, goals, and implementation. As he explained after describing the Army's mobilization planning in his 1931 annual report as Chief of Staff:

> *Our responsibility in this matter is too great to permit the inclusion in our plans of any proposed policy of whose successful operation in war we do not feel we can give assurance. Certainly, our plans are the result of honest effort. They are developing along lines that we believe experience had pointed out and present conditions dictate.*

The very fact that MacArthur had set the General Staff to work creating war mobilization plans in 1931 is a good example of one of his great strengths as a planner. He was consistent in his ability to think beyond the short-term demands of his position and consider the long-term needs of his organizations. "[H]e had great vision," said Robert White who served in MacArthur's headquarters in WWII. "He always looked into the future, what's the next step, how are we going to outmaneuver the Japanese on it, what is their strength, what is their weakness."

MacArthur always seemed to be at least one step ahead. Early in 1945, while the battle for the Philippines still raged and his staff had not yet even begun to plan the invasion of Japan, MacArthur, believing that Japan would surrender before the year was out, was already considering the proper priorities of the occupation. Later, just days after the outbreak of the Korean War, he set his strategic planners to work on the plan that would come to fruition at Inchon.

General LeGrande Diller, who served as MacArthur's public relations officer in the Philippines and later in Australia, quickly discovered that "he was a meticulous planner." Said Diller:

> *I found out how it was that I was called to his office when I had never met him before. He had figured that perhaps there would be a war and perhaps he would be called to active duty and perhaps he would be put in command, which all materialized. And the book, the Army Register, which had a record of all of us officers, had several officers with notes by their names and I found that book and realized that he had made this study and six of us were called to his headquarters the day after he was recalled by President Roosevelt.*

As in his operations, MacArthur preached and practiced speed in strategic planning. He was not interested in spending months developing perfect plans or creating shelves of manuals; he was focused on creating reasonable, executable plans that could be adjusted if and when the need arose. This efficiency in planning enabled him to conserve resources and speed operations.

An example of the benefits of this practice can be seen in the rollout of the Civilian Conservation Corps (CCC) during the Great Depression. The CCC was one of most successful of President Roosevelt's New Deal programs; it put more than 3.4 million young men to work on public parks, roads, utilities, and erosion-control projects between 1933 and 1942.

Roosevelt, who had committed to have 250,000 workers on the job by July 1, 1933, enlisted MacArthur's assistance in mobilizing the CCC. The Army created a plan, which was competed and approved a week before the legislation was approved on March 31. It also managed the enrollment of recruits, put them through a two-week training program, and delivered them to their assigned work camps.

Between May 12 and July 1, the Army delivered 275,000 CCC workers to their work sites in 47 states. Wrote MacArthur biographer D. Clayton James:

> *The huge operation involved over 200 trains and 3,600 Army vehicles; the youths were supplied with 1,225,000 pairs of trousers and 1,700,000 towels drawn from quartermaster depots; sites were cleared and construction was completed on 1,330 work camps.*

Compared with the Army's mobilization effort in WWI, it had deployed over 100,000 more men in two-thirds of the time. The successful CCC effort proved the efficacy of MacArthur's mobilization plans.

The Army's mobilization plans of the early 1930s offer a final cautionary lesson. They were no longer viable by the outbreak of WWII; they did not account for the new technologies and mechanized equipment that became standard in the late 1930s and early 1940s. The lesson: No plan is timeless. When conditions change, plans must change, too.

"Certainly, our plans are the result of honest effort."

Reflection Questions:

- Are you dedicating time to the consideration of long-term objectives?

- How can your organization simultaneously streamline its planning process and increase the accuracy of its plans?

Chapter 29

Invest in Training

Leaders are responsible for the preparedness of their followers, and training is a foundational element of preparedness. Although training is essential to the successful execution of strategy, leaders often mistakenly treat it as an ancillary activity: one that can be reduced when budgets are tight and ignored when its need is not obvious. Ironically, those are exactly the times when training is most important.

In the midst of the Depression in the early 1930s, military preparedness was not high on the list of priorities of the nation's leaders. In contrast, Chief of Staff MacArthur was relentless in his pursuit of training. He warned:

> *From the beginning of warfare, professional skill and discipline have invariably been most important, and frequently the decisive factors in battle. To quote instances would imply a necessity to argue the obvious. Yet strangely enough this outstanding lesson of each of our own as well as of all other wars has invariably been the one most speedily forgotten by our people during years of peace. It has been the history of the American Army that adequate opportunity for its proper training has habitually been, except in war, injudiciously curtailed.*

MacArthur approached the imperative for training from three levels. In his mind, the most important was that which was devoted to leadership development. "The first essential of an efficient training system is a strong corps of highly qualified Regular officers," wrote the Chief of Staff in 1934. "[T]he lack of skill in the officer directly endangers the lives of followers and comrades, as well as his own...An army without trained leaders is a contradiction in terms."

As superintendent of West Point, MacArthur had devoted all his attention to the development of officer corps. As chief of staff, he was a staunch advocate of the Army's educational system and all of its institutions. "Our educational process is progressive, practical, and comprehensive," he said. He explained that officers first received the technical skills required to execute their assigned jobs and then, through the General Service School and Army War College, the broader education needed to prepare them for higher levels of command.

MacArthur's second priority was the training of the enlisted personnel of the Regular Army. He wrote:

> *Foremost among the considerations governing the War Department's purposes is the insistent need for maximum technical proficiency among a reasonably strong corps of professional soldiers. Modern warfare constantly increases in complexity. Weapons have grown more complicated in design and require the utmost in technical skill for their effective use. These multiply the potential combat power of the individual and this circumstance automatically permits and even dictates greater dispersion on the battlefield. Compact masses are a battle characteristic of the past, and close control, obtained by personal contact, is no longer possible. Effective results will obtain only where each soldier is a master of technique and so thoroughly indoctrinated in correct tactical methods as to function satisfactorily under conditions of relative isolation and independence.*

Finally, MacArthur turned his attention to the training of civilians. In business terms, he was concerned with overall competency of the labor pool from which his organization would draw job candidates. MacArthur knew that the nation depended on citizen-soldiers in time of war, and he wanted to ensure that they would be prepared when the call to duty came.

MacArthur rallied support in Congress for the funding needed to build a fully staffed and well-trained National Guard and Officer Reserve Corps. He wrote:

> *It is especially important that these be maintained as properly administered organizations characterized by dependable discipline and sound basic training, since they are intended for early support of the Regular Army in emergency. Moreover, the Guard should be furnished as rapidly as possible, with weapons and equipment of the latest types and thoroughly practiced in their use. But the special conditions under which the Guard is maintained sharply differentiates the character of its training from that of the Regular Army. The brief periods available to the Guard for training must be employed toward attainment of its principal objective—production of basically sound units.*

Leaders should also be sure not to overlook their own roles as teachers. Their own behavior and actions can help develop their followers' skills. Here is how General Charles West interpreted MacArthur's habit of conducting long analytical monologues in front of his staff:

> *It was a trait, but I almost wonder whether it wasn't a trait that he developed over the years in training young officers, like the Eisenhowers who served him, how to think through a military problem and come to a logical conclusion. I don't think he was presuming to take [senior officers] and teach them how to do a staff study and come to some conclusions. But I think maybe one of the things he was doing unconsciously (and I think he did a great many things unconsciously) here was showing them what his thought processes were in order to educate them into how he wanted them to approach problems with him.*

"Training distinguishes an army from an armed mob."

Reflection Questions:

- Are the training needs of each level of your organization's employees defined and delivered?

- What is your most important skill, and how can you teach it to your followers?

Chapter 30

Develop Management Depth

In recent years, middle managers have often been maligned. They have been treated as organizational dead wood and their ranks have often been mercilessly downsized. Leaders of large organizations sometimes forget that managers convey and execute strategies. They represent an organization's frontline leadership.

MacArthur needed no convincing that managers were a most important component of an organization. In the early 1930s, in response to a bill calling for forced furloughs on half-pay for a substantial number of active officers, he told the House Military Affairs Committee:

> *The foundation of our National Defense system is the Regular Army, and the foundation of the Regular Army is the officer. He is the soul of the system; if you have to cut everything out of the National Defense Act, the last element should be the officer corps. If you had to discharge every soldier, if you had to do away with everything else, I would still professionally advise you to keep those 12,000 officers. They are the mainspring of the whole mechanism; each one of them would be worth a thousand men at the beginning of a war. They are the only ones who can take this heterogeneous group and make it a homogenous group.*

In fact, MacArthur successfully conducted a running battle to maintain the size and quality of the officer corps throughout his tenure as Chief of Staff. "An efficient and sufficient corps of officers means the difference between victory and defeat," he said, explaining that without the officer corps to train and lead the many civilians that would be drafted into the military in case of war, the creation of an effective fighting force was impossible.

MacArthur identified the frontline leadership that managers provide as their most important job. He said:

> *[T]he difficulties of retaining control of fighting lines constantly increase. But this control is the basic function of all commanders, and they must not give way to the tendency to establish themselves as mere message centers in a complicated system of signal communication. Theirs is a task of leadership—continuous, energetic, and courageous leadership—and if they become immersed in the staff problems of battle, they will abandon the Army to leaderless effort and almost certain defeat. Constant insistence on these essentials and constant training in applicable method and doctrine are necessary to insure efficiency.*

In the 1930s, Chief of Staff MacArthur supported the acceleration of the officer promotion rate and pay scales. These policy revisions were aimed at maintaining a high-quality officer corps. His own career notwithstanding, even the best officers were reaching ranks above colonel only a few years before their retirement. MacArthur wanted to ensure that the Army maximized the usefulness of these officers by increasing the time they served in senior positions. He used better pay to attract and retain better officers.

In addition to his concerns about the career advancement and compensation of managers, MacArthur recognized the danger and the stress to which his officers were exposed. In WWII, when General Kenney flew a reconnaissance mission over enemy positions, he returned to headquarters and "spent the next ten minutes listening while General MacArthur bawled me out for flying around where there might be some Japs. He said he had decided that he needed me to look after the Air Force and that, from now on, I would stay south of the Owen Stanley Mountains unless I got direct permission from him otherwise."

Physician Roger Egeberg was unable to get MacArthur to agree to even a standard physical examination, but MacArthur did give him an important assignment. When he "hired" Egeberg, he said:

I need somebody to get to know the officers of this headquarters. They are under a kind of tension which you don't often see. In a combat zone, tension can be relieved by fighting, but that is not the case here. Their troubles are more difficult to get at here, so your job is to find out what makes them react. Tell me if you see officers who need rest or a change of assignment.

Lest MacArthur's largesse and concern for his officers seem soft-hearted, it should be noted that he had good reasons for wanting the best available officers. "[T]here can be no hope of preparing efficiently, or of winning in actual campaigns, without the skilled leadership of trained and devoted officers," he said. And MacArthur was intent on winning.

In addition to winning, MacArthur also placed great demands on his staff. He worked long hours and expected them to be available whenever he needed them. He also required high intelligence, complete loyalty, and energetic initiative. Any officer who did not live up to these expectations was quickly given a new assignment elsewhere.

"They are the mainspring of the whole mechanism..."

Reflection Questions:

- Are the spans of control assigned your managers reasonable?

- Are your organization's managers focused on the primary job of executing strategy?

Chapter 31

Delegate Whenever Possible

Micromanagers rarely make great leaders. They bog down in details and risk missing the forest for the trees. It is obviously impossible for leaders to do it all, especially in large organizations. Good leaders avoid this trap by learning to delegate.

Besides being an unavoidable necessity in the leadership of large organizations, delegation offers a variety of benefits. It enables leaders to dedicate time and effort to high-priority tasks. It empowers followers and demonstrates the trust of the leader. It enhances the leadership potential, skills, and confidence of those chosen as delegates. And it creates organizational growth and improved performance through the simultaneous achievement of multiple goals.

MacArthur was an expert at delegation, and the officers that worked for him appreciated the confidence and trust that that implied. President Dwight Eisenhower said, "[MacArthur] was a rewarding man to work for. When he gave an assignment, he never asked any questions; he never cared what kind of hours were kept; his only requirement was that the work be done."

Senior aide Laurence Bunker, who served under MacArthur during the Japanese occupation, also noted "the General's unusual capacity of being willing to delegate authority along with responsibility. In other words, if he gave a man a job, he also gave him adequate authority to carry it out, and then held him responsible for the way he did it and the end result. He didn't nag him while he was on the job. He gave him the job and looked to him to finish it."

Not only was MacArthur a delegator; he was convinced that the ability to delegate was a critical skill for to senior leaders. He once told Bunker:

> *Up through the ranks until [an officer] becomes a division commander, he knows every one of his officers personally and knows all about them. He knows their personal problems; he understands why they function this way, why they do things this way instead of another. But when he goes from division commander to corps commander, he is dealing with too many people, and this is particularly true as far as the rank and file are concerned. He can't possibly keep track of the individual and be concerned about the individual welfare and individual problems in his command. He's got to deal with things at a higher level, and he just cannot spend his time and mental energy on those problems. So there are very few men who have that capacity to drop the personal approach to all these problems, which is an asset for them in the earlier ranks, and go on to this higher attitude. So we have a lot of corps commanders who are still really good division commanders.*

Effective delegation requires that leaders ensure that they are assigning tasks to people who are able and prepared to successfully accomplish them. In MacArthur's headquarters in WWII, "the doctrine of completed staff work" was one way that delegates knew what was required of them. The author of the doctrine is unknown, but the memo circulated through the Army in 1942:

Completed Staff Work

The doctrine of "completed staff work" is a doctrine of this office.

"Completed staff work" is the study of a problem and presentation of a solution, by a staff officer, in such form that all that remains to be done on the part of the head of the staff division, or the commander, is to indicate his approval or disapproval of the completed action. The words "completed action" are emphasized because the more difficult the problem is, the more the tendency is to present the problem to the chief in piece-meal fashion. It is your duty as a staff officer to work out the details. You should not consult your chief in the determination of these details, no matter how perplexing they may be. You may and should consult other staff officers. The product, whether it involved the pronouncement of a new policy of effects or an established one, should, when presented to the chief for approval or disapproval, be worked out in finished form.

The impulse, which often comes to the inexperienced staff officer to ask the chief what to do, recurs more often when the problem is difficult. It is accompanied by a feeling of mental frustration. It is so easy to ask the chief what to do, and it appears so easy for him to answer. Resist that impulse. You will succumb to it only if you do not know your job. It is your job to advise your chief what he ought to do, not to ask him what you ought to do. He needs answers, not questions. Your job is to study, write, restudy and rewrite until you have evolved a single proposed action—the best one of all you have considered. Your chief merely approves or disapproves.

Do not worry your chief with long explanations and memoranda. Writing a memorandum to your chief does not constitute completed staff work, but writing a memorandum for your chief to send to someone else does. Your views should be placed before him in finished form so that he can make them his views simply by signing his name. In most instances, completed staff work results in a single document prepared for the signature of the chief, without accompanying comment. If the proper result is reached, the chief will usually recognize it at once. If he wants comment or explanation, he will ask for it.

The theory of completed staff work does not preclude a "rough draft" but the rough draft must not be a half-baked idea. It must be complete in every respect except that it lacks the requisite number of copies and need not be neat. But a rough draft must not be used as an excuse for shifting to the chief the burden of formulating the action.

The "completed staff work" theory may result in more work for the staff officer, but it results in more freedom for the chief. This is as it should be. Further, it accomplishes two things:

- The chief is protected from half-baked ideas, voluminous memoranda, and immature oral presentments.
- The staff officer who has a real idea to sell is enabled more readily to find a market.

When you have finished your "completed staff work," the final test is this: If you were the chief, would you be willing to sign the paper you have prepared, and stake your professional reputation on its being right? If the answer is in the negative, take it back and work it over, because it is not yet "completed staff work."

The doctrine emphasizes a final point regarding delegation. Delegation, as MacArthur well understood, does not necessarily require an abdication of decision-making. Leaders are ultimately responsible for the actions of an organization. They should delegate work freely, but they should also retain their power to review and approve significant decisions.

"...there are very few men who have that capacity to drop the personal approach...and go on to this higher attitude."

Reflection Questions:

- Can you devote more time to your most important responsibilities by delegating?

- Are your subordinates equipped with the skills and resources they need to successfully complete delegated tasks?

Chapter 32

Manage People Positively

Great leaders tend to be motivational experts. They might choose to use positive methods or negative methods of motivation, or (most often) some combination of both. But no matter the type of organization in which they lead, they are able to create and maintain motivated and energized workforces.

MacArthur was an expert people manager. One measure of his success was the fact that the more closely people worked with him, the more they admired and respected him. His greatest defenders were often his own staff officers. His greatest critics, on the other hand, tended to be people who either did not know him at all or not with any degree of intimacy.

One reason for his success was MacArthur's ability to understand the needs of others. Paul Rogers, chief clerk in the General's office throughout WWII, observed, "MacArthur was a master at motivating subordinates. He could reach each man's character to find the most basic center of appeal. MacArthur played them all: ambition, self-fulfillment, glory, desire to serve. In each man, great or small, he found the core of character and used it."

On occasion, MacArthur resorted to the stick to motivate his followers, but his inclination and preference was always the carrot. His experiences as a combat leader in WWI convinced him that positive motivational tactics worked best in armies that were largely comprised of citizens.

When he assumed command at West Point on his return, he said:

> *Discipline no longer required extreme methods. Men generally needed only to be told what to do, rather than to be forced by the fear of consequence of failure. The great numbers involved made it impossible to apply the old rigid methods which had been so successful when battle lines were not so extensive.*

MacArthur suggested that the Army needed officers "possessing an intimate understanding of the mechanics of human feeling, a comprehensive grasp of world and national affairs, and a liberalization of conception which amounts to a change in his psychology of command." In other words, the rigid authoritarianism and negative motivation of the Old Army had become outdated.

It is easy to see how MacArthur applied this thinking in his personal management style. Earlier than many experts, he perceived the mutuality that characterizes the relationship between leaders and followers. In a 1949 statement, he wrote:

> *Unappreciated perhaps by many of our countrymen is the time honored and battle proved understanding among and between soldiers that confidence, respect and loyalty must extend downward as well as upward, in thought and in deed, both from and to the commander; and this "two-way" principle applies with equal force, be the level that of the high command or the foxhole.*

MacArthur applied his phenomenal memory to enhance his people skills. He won over many people simply by virtue of remembering their names or some small detail or connection, and/or greeting them warmly.

Praise, a no-cost form of recognition that too many leaders neglect, was another of MacArthur's motivational tactics. In December 1944, for example, two privates in the 11th Airborne requested an audience with the five-star general to find out why their division's accomplishments had not received more press attention. MacArthur met with them, explained that he did not want to publicize their unit's position, and provided a message of praise for the division and its commander to deliver on their return to combat.

MacArthur, realizing that partiality and discrimination were demotivators, was a firm adherent of the merit system. In WWII, when General

Kenney recommended 32-year-old Paul Wurtsmith for promotion to brigadier general, there were complaints about his youth. MacArthur reportedly snapped, "We promote them here for efficiency, not for age."

This emphasis on merit extended to decorations and awards. In 1943, MacArthur withheld approval for one Medal of Honor candidate on the grounds that, "Nothing is so injurious to morale as a belief that favoritism and privilege are exercised by high authority in such matters—I deprecate such action on the part of officers who thus seek to avoid proper command channels and recommend that the War Department discourage such action as being subversive of military discipline."

These kinds of tactics enabled MacArthur to coax peak performances from his followers. Robert Danforth, who served as Commandant of Cadets while MacArthur was head of West Point, described it like this:

> *[His] was a gifted leadership, a leadership that kept you at a respectful distance, yet at the same time took you as an esteemed member of his team, and very quickly had you working harder than you had ever worked before in your life, just because of the loyalty, admiration and respect in which you held him.*

MacArthur himself simply summarized his methods in this description of his first company command:

> *By praising them when they were good and shaming them when they were bad, by raising their pride and developing their sense of self-respect, I soon began to convince them they were the best of the lot.*

"A general is just as good or just as bad as the troops under his command make him. Mine were great!"

Reflection Questions:

- Do you spend at least as much time praising employees as you do criticizing them?

- What no-cost methods of recognition and reward can your organization provide its managers to help them motivate their followers?

Chapter 33

Adopt the MacArthur Tenets

In the early 1960s, William Addleman Ganoe wrote a memoir of his service 40 years earlier as MacArthur's chief of staff at West Point. Ganoe had gone on to become a noted Army historian. He wrote the first history of the Army, worked at the Army War College, and went to Europe in WWII as the chief historian in that theater.

It appears that Ganoe first turned the people-management traits he had observed in MacArthur into the list of 17 questions called "The MacArthur Tenets" during WWII. He wrote of creating them with General Jacob Devers, a noted strategist and senior leader. Ganoe said:

> *[W]hen General Devers in London was disturbed over the bad results his subordinate officers in the field were getting with their soldiers, I showed him the pattern; he at once grasped the idea of sending it out over his signature to colonels and lieutenant colonels. In order not to be preachy, we put it in the form of questions.*

Devers reported that morale "had gone up unbelievably" after the questions were circulated. Ganoe himself was convinced of their usefulness. He examined the records of other leaders and reported, "I found all those who had no troubles from their charges, from General Sun Tzsu in China long ago to George Eastman of Kodak fame, followed the same pattern almost to the letter."

These are the questions that Ganoe distilled from MacArthur's leadership at West Point, as he published them in the long out-of-print memoir,

MacArthur Close-Up:

1. Do I heckle my subordinates or strengthen and encourage them?
2. Do I use moral courage in getting rid of subordinates who have proven themselves beyond doubt to be unfit?
3. Have I done all in my power by encouragement, incentive and spur to salvage the weak and erring?
4. Do I know by NAME and CHARACTER a maximum number of subordinates for whom I am responsible? Do I know them intimately?
5. Am I thoroughly familiar with the technique, necessities, objectives, and administration of my job?
6. Do I lose my temper at individuals?
7. Do I act in such a way as to make my subordinates WANT to follow me?
8. Do I delegate tasks which should be mine?
9. Do I arrogate everything to myself and delegate nothing?
10. Do I develop my subordinates by placing on each one as much responsibility as he can stand?
11. Am I interested in the personal welfare of each of my subordinates, as if he were a member of my family?
12. Have I the calmness of voice and manner to inspire confidence, or am I inclined to irascibility and excitability?
13. Am I a constant example to my subordinates in character, dress, deportment, and courtesy?
14. Am I inclined to be nice to my superiors and mean to my subordinates?
15. Is my door open to my subordinates?
16. Do I think more of POSITION than JOB?
17. Do I correct a subordinate in the presence of others?

The MacArthur Tenets emphasize a humanist approach to leaders' relationships with their followers. They imply interpersonal exchanges based on respect, caring, and loyalty. At the same time, they recognize that followers also have obligations in terms of performance and results. If they do not fulfill those obligations, leaders must act to resolve the shortfall. Adopt the MacArthur Tenets as a litmus test to measure and balance both demands.

Chapter 34

Do More With Less

Achievement of any organizational goal requires resources. A manufacturer requires labor and material to produce a finished product; a non-profit needs contributions and volunteers to provide its services; an army needs troops and weaponry to win battles. Leaders rarely have all the resources they require to achieve their goals. They must learn to do more with less.

In the early stages of both WWII and Korea, MacArthur faced severe shortages of both men and equipment. His creative responses to shortages earned him a well-deserved reputation as a leader who (as D. Clayton James put it) could win with "relatively meager logistical support."

The most serious shortages that MacArthur faced were in manpower, a condition that is common in many of today's organizations. In an August 1950 conference with Ambassador Averill Harriman and representatives of the Joint Chiefs of Staff, MacArthur declared: "Our main problem now is one of replacements. We have the cadres here and all we need are the fillers. Men who are veterans need only have a rifle, and we can handle the rest. Our system of replacement is antiquated. It must be made more elastic!"

MacArthur stretched his fighting forces in Korea in two ways. First, he moved his best troops into the front lines. In the early days of the war, he moved every trained soldier in Japan and in the Army service units forward. He covered the shortages by authorizing the expansion of Japan's national police force to ensure continued order during the occupation. As he had done in Australia in WWII, he also recruited civilians for noncombatant jobs, thus covering the ensuing shortage of service troops. The Army later estimated that without the Japanese workers, the Korean War would have required as many as 250,000 additional troops.

MacArthur followed the same tactic in planning Inchon. Realizing that the success of the invasion would hinge on the first day and that his own units were stretched beyond their capacity, he reached outside the Army. MacArthur knew that the Marine Corps was threatened with budget cuts and likely looking for an opportunity to prove their value, so he asked them for help. His request was quickly answered; ultimately, it was 1st Marine Division that spearheaded the initial landing at Inchon. The veteran unit, which had fought at Guadalcanal and Okinawa, was arguably the most experienced amphibious invasion force in the world.

Second, MacArthur bolstered his Korean combat units by pairing experienced solders with newly trained soldiers. He conceived the so-called Buddy System. Struggling to slow and stop the North Korean onslaught in the first months of war, MacArthur asked South Korea to recruit young men for the war. In August and September of 1950, almost 9,000 Korean men were trained in Japan. The KATUSA (Koreans Attached to the U.S. Army) were then paired with experienced soldiers in the 7th Division, which was fighting to hold the Pusan Perimeter.

In Korea, MacArthur also skirted the "no-war" constitution clause he had been instrumental in creating by enlisting Japanese personnel in the military effort. He utilized Japanese transportation crews in ports and railroad operations. Japanese military experts also served as consultants in SCAP headquarters and the 8th Army.

MacArthur could be just as creative when it came to equipment needs. After the Japanese surrender, U.S. military budgets predictably shrank, and there was no new equipment sent to MacArthur in the Pacific. In response, in 1947, MacArthur instituted Operation Roll-up.

Roll-up was designed to collect and reclaim the millions of tons of Army equipment that remained scattered throughout the Pacific after WWII. This equipment was staged in depots and was then sent to Japan, where it served a double purpose. MacArthur supported the struggling Japanese economy by putting Japanese workers and plants to work refurbishing the equipment. He also resupplied his four divisions at the same time; Roll-up provided 90 percent of their armaments and 75 percent of their motor vehicles.

At the outbreak of the Korean War, MacArthur accelerated Roll-up. According to the Army's official history, in the first four months of war, Roll-up provided 489,000 small arms; 1,418 artillery pieces; 34,316 pieces of fire-control equipment; 743 combat vehicles; and 15,000 general-purpose vehicles. D. Clayton James said, "Equipment for MacArthur's ground forces was made up almost entirely of World War II vehicles, guns, and other items that had been overhauled in Operation Roll-up."

"Because of lack of funds, multiplicity of types is to be avoided, and whenever practical, simple, relatively inexpensive items are to be preferred over the more elaborate and expensive varieties."

Reflection Questions:

- Can you staff a new project without new hires by redeploying your existing workforce?

- What existing equipment within your organization is unused, and how can it be repurposed?

Chapter 35

Avoid Human Losses

No matter what type of results that an organization pursues—profits, battlefield victories, or charitable good works—people are the one indispensable factor in their attainment. Thus, every organizational goal exacts a human cost, and every great leader considers and (whenever possible) minimizes that cost.

MacArthur clearly understood that wars could not be won without troops. He was also well aware that the human cost of war was tallied in casualties—dead and wounded men and women. Hints of the depth of his concern over this cost can be seen in the fact that during WWII, MacArthur started work each day by examining the casualty reports. General Kenney said, "MacArthur would get the casualty list at the end of every 24-hour period, and the tears would roll down his cheeks if one man was killed." In both WWII and Korea, he sent personally signed letters to the families of those who died.

Throughout his career, MacArthur never hesitated to order troops into battle; he was first and foremost a warrior. But he was also vehemently opposed to the unnecessary loss of life. During the Pearl Harbor Conference of 1944, President Roosevelt expressed his concern about the casualty rates that would be incurred in the liberation of the Philippines. MacArthur replied:

Mr. President, my losses would not be heavy, anymore than they have been in the past. The days of the frontal attack should be over. Modern infantry weapons are too deadly, and frontal assault is only for mediocre commanders. Good commanders do not turn in heavy losses.

By and large, MacArthur lived up to his words. The total casualties incurred after MacArthur took command of the SW Pacific Theater were less than those incurred in the Battle of the Bulge alone. Correspondent William Dunn said:

I've always said that there are thousands of Americans who came back to their families from fighting under General MacArthur because he talked the bloodiest war you've ever heard, when he talked to you he practically dripped blood but he didn't fight that way, ever. He never lost a man that wasn't necessary…

Aside from the obvious benefit of minimizing the loss of life and suffering, MacArthur's attitude and practices enabled him to conserve troops—the most important assets of his organization—and assets that were often in short supply. They also enhanced his reputation and cache with those who fought under his command. Colonel Henry Burgess, who served under MacArthur in the 11th Airborne during WWII, explained:

I felt a great deal of confidence in the reputation which he had of trying to save the lives of his troops. He had adopted a policy ever since World War I, when he was subjected to the great mass trench warfare onslaughts, of trying to bypass enemies' strong points and that was the whole scheme of the island-hopping that came up through the area of New Guinea into the Philippines and across the Pacific area in between there.

Strategy, as discussed in Part Two, was one way in which MacArthur minimized human losses. In a 1948 letter, he wrote:

The lessons of military history point to two great fallacies common to all peoples of all time—the tendency to place undue reliance for victory upon the power of arms alone, and the failure to measure victory's gain by its human and material cost. For victory, as well, is dependent upon the spiritual strength of the human resources involved and the qualities of leadership dedicated to their employment—and non-essential costs bring undue tragedy to loved ones bereaved, and unnecessary weakness to future power in the advance.

Estimated casualty rates were an important consideration in MacArthur's strategic planning. General Carlos Romulo, a Filipino who served in MacArthur's headquarters, said:

> *I heard him say before any operation to the Staff, "How many casualties do you think we're going to have in this operation?" That was his first thought: How many casualties? And when they said, they counted so much that was it, he said, "No, that's too many. Let's think of another operation."*

MacArthur also used intelligence to avoid situations with high potential losses. Dr. Paul Robinson said:

> *I think that the commander who places his troops up against an obstacle, that is, one obviously too difficult for them, certainly is going to have heavy losses. That is the thing that a commander can avoid if he has proper intelligence...This was where General MacArthur excelled. Not only that, but he demanded that kind of activity, I think, among his commanders too.*

MacArthur did make sure that his field officers shared his attitude. Robinson continued:

> *He was not tolerant of casualties...Before they came to Leyte, there was an officer who was relieved from a division command because of his large number of losses.*

General Joseph Swing remembered MacArthur telling him, "Joe, we don't do it over here the way the Marines do it or the way they do it over in Europe. We use a little military common sense on how we get our men killed. We don't do it by massive brute force. Anybody can fight that way." MacArthur's message was clear and as Swing said, "I tried to fight that way too."

"Success in war depends on men, not money."

Reflection Questions:

- Do you weigh the human costs of your strategies and tactics before you act on them?

- Do any of your managers consider employees expendable?

Chapter 36

Manage Upward

Almost all leaders are also subordinates. The heads of corporations and nonprofits typically answer to their boards of directors; military chiefs of staff answer to heads of state. That is why in order to achieve their objectives and advance through the ranks, leaders must manage their superiors as well as their subordinates.

MacArthur is perhaps most remembered today for his notable failure, whether intentional or not, in managing President Truman. But that dénouement, which may well be Truman's failure more than MacArthur's, belies the reality: MacArthur was an expert at managing up. He knew that managing his superiors well was as essential as managing his troops, and that his career as well as the resources for his campaigns depended on the maintenance of solid, working relationships all the way up the chain of command.

Biographer D. Clayton James surveyed MacArthur's relationships with the heads of state and concluded:

> *Except for Truman, whom he personally met only once, for a few hours on Wake Island in 1950, the general's connections with American, Philippine, Australian, and Japanese heads of state, from 1930 to 1951 rank as his most harmonious working relationships beyond the inner circle of his own staff.*

President Hoover became a lifelong friend and ally. Although MacArthur opposed President Roosevelt's politics, Roosevelt had tremendous confidence in him, and they worked together quite effectively. Philippine President Manuel Quezon and Australian Prime Minister John Curtin also held MacArthur in high regard.

As in his relationships with subordinates, MacArthur preferred the carrot to the stick in dealing with his superiors. There are innumerable examples that show he was not above using his communication skills to flatter a superior. In WWII, for example, when Secretary of War Henry Stimson praised MacArthur for the working relationship he had established with the Australian government, MacArthur replied: "It has always been one of the guiding principles of my life to merit the commendation of the Secretary of War, and in the present instance this is peculiarly accentuated by my long personal association and deep respect and admiration for him."

General William Beiderlinden reports how MacArthur successfully managed three members of the Senate who visited Japan:

[I]t was my job to go to the Imperial Hotel to pick them up. On the way over to the Dai Ichi Building one senator said, "Now, let's get together on this. The thing we've got to do is to tell General MacArthur that he's got to quit spending so much money. The United States taxpayer is not going to take putting out one million dollars a day here for these Japanese people. We've put out plenty, and he's got to cut it down." They all agreed.

I took them up and introduced them to General MacArthur...he would know everything about any guy who came in to see him. He would know all things about him, and he would mention these things and mention people that he knew. About two or two and a half hours later...I went down to meet them on the elevator, and they said, "You know, we didn't know all this. MacArthur's right. He needs that money. He needs more than what he's getting."

MacArthur completely hypnotized all three of them.

As with subordinates, when MacArthur could not get what he needed from a superior with a carrot, he had no problem turning to the stick. The MacArthur archives are full of his "requests for clarification." When faced with an order with which he disagreed, he would use a request for clarification to detail his objections and attempt to convince his superiors to change their minds.

If the case was urgent enough in his mind and MacArthur could not convince his superiors to act as he wished, he would apply external pressure. As you'll see in Chapter 48, he would enlist the press and public opinion on his behalf. This, of course, can be a dangerous game, and in the case of the Truman-MacArthur controversy, it was MacArthur's use of public channels that proved to be the ultimate cause of his recall.

Although MacArthur always maintained his independence of thought and would aggressively push his prerogative to challenge his superiors' actions to its limits, he never completely rebelled. When MacArthur's challenges were overruled, he accepted his orders. When Hoover ordered him to roust the Bonus Marchers, he obeyed. When Roosevelt ordered him to leave the Philippines, he obeyed.

In his dealings with Truman, MacArthur certainly subverted the wishes of his Commander-in-Chief. But, he also used the chaos of the administration's contradictory policies and orders to support and justify his actions. If Truman had instead issued him clear, direct, and final orders, it would have been out of character for MacArthur to refuse to obey.

"I have been a soldier for 52 years. I have in that time, to the best of my ability, carried out every order that was ever given me."

Reflection Questions:

- How can you work more effectively with your superiors?

- Do your subordinates have an established and clear process to challenge your orders and decisions?

★★★★★

PART FIVE

PERSONAL TRAITS OF A LEADER

Chapter 37

Live Your Values

Duty, honor, and country are the three values specified in West Point's famous motto. The motto was selected in 1898, just one year before MacArthur entered the academy. He embraced it as a cadet and worked to embody its values for the rest of his life.

The importance that MacArthur assigned to values was clear in the famous final speech he gave at West Point on May 12, 1962. "Duty-honor-country," he said. "Those three hallowed words reverently dictate what you ought to be, what you can be, what you will be." He went on to explain to the cadets the significance of values and their power to provide balance to a leader's approach and actions:

> *They teach you to be proud and unbending in honest failure, but humble and gentle in success; not to substitute words for actions, not to seek the path of comfort, but to face the stress and spur of difficulty and challenge; to learn to stand up in the storm, but to have compassion on those who fall; to master yourself before you seek to master others; to have a heart that is clean, a goal that is high; to learn to laugh, yet never forget how to weep; to reach into the future, yet never neglect the past; to be serious, yet never to take yourself too seriously; to be modest so that you will remember the simplicity of true greatness, the open mind of true wisdom, the meekness of true strength.*

MacArthur was taught the importance of values from a very early age. His parents inculcated a simple value set that emphasized patriotism and doing "what was right," no matter the personal consequences. Having grown up in the Army, it was only a short leap from family values to the professional values of an officer.

MacArthur's values guided him in decision-making in both war and peace. His successful resistance against all plans to bypass the Philippines in the effort to win the war against Japan was clearly values-related. In July 1944, President Roosevelt called MacArthur to Pearl Harbor to hear his views on how to best reach Japan. MacArthur argued the strategic and psychological advantages, and then made the ethical case. There was "a moral obligation," according to MacArthur. Honor demanded that 17 million Filipinos and the captive American troops not be abandoned yet again. Three days later at a press conference, FDR said, "We are going to get the Philippines back and without question General MacArthur will take part in it."

Values also contributed to MacArthur's ability to stay the course when the implementation of a decision became difficult. General Alexander Haig, the former Secretary of State who served in SCAP headquarters during the occupation of Japan and in Korea, says, "One of General MacArthur's greatest strengths was his supreme confidence that he derived from the depth of his convictions."

Values were not restricted to individuals in MacArthur's view. He made every effort to disseminate them throughout the organizations he led. His institutionalization of West Point's famous honor code is a good example. "The highest standards of honor were to be demanded as the only solid foundation for a military career," said MacArthur, "A code of individual conduct which would maintain the reputation and well-being of the whole—a personal responsibility to his mates, to his community, and above all to his country."

Nor were values, such as duty, to be suspended when times got tough. Paul Rogers, who as chief clerk in MacArthur's headquarters during WWII had an intimate view, remembered MacArthur as a sensitive, quiet man. "All of this notwithstanding, he could be as brittle as obsidian where duty was concerned, ruthless in the demand that soldiers fight to the death if necessary," said Rogers. "MacArthur would say quietly, 'You will do your duty. Perform, and I will forget it all and reward you. Persist, and I will humiliate you. But you will perform your duty.'"

MacArthur equated good leadership with the consistency of values. He once told an officer enrolled in Army's Command and General Staff College: "Moral courage—true leadership—is based upon a fundamental but simple philosophy—to do what you think is right as opposed to what you think is wrong irrespective of the popularity or unpopularity which may result, and always with the realization that being human you may be wrong in your decision." Values, of course, are how we determine what is right.

It is not hard to imagine what MacArthur's reaction would be to the rash of corporate scandals in the first few years of the new millennium. In a speech to the Salvation Army given on December 12, 1951, MacArthur warned, "History fails to record a single precedent in which nations subject to moral decay have not passed into political and economic decline. There has been either a spiritual reawakening to overcome the moral lapse, or a progressive deterioration leading to the ultimate national disaster."

"...what you ought to be, what you can be, what you will be."

Reflection Questions:

- What personal values guide your actions?

- What values guide your organization?

Chapter 38

Pursue the Ideal

Many people think of idealism as a luxury of youth. They mistakenly believe that there is no room for idealism within a realist's world view and associate it with naiveté and lost causes. MacArthur, who experienced a lifetime on the frontlines of war, saw realism at its worst. Yet, he was an idealist, and he remained one until the end of his life,.

One of MacArthur's favorite quotations, which was framed and displayed in his office in Tokyo, started: "Youth is not a time of life—it is a state of mind. Nobody grows old by merely living a number of years; people grow old only by deserting their ideals." The words came from a prose poem written in the early 1900s by Samuel Ullman, a civic leader and educator from Alabama.

At an American Legion banquet on his 75th birthday, MacArthur gave a speech that paraphrased and elaborated on Ullman's poem. He said, in part:

> *You are as young as your faith, as old as your doubt; as young as your self-confidence, as old as your fear; as young as your hope, as old as your despair. In the central place of every heart there is a recording chamber; so long as it receives messages of beauty, hope, cheer and courage, so long are you young. When the wires are all down and your heart is covered with the snows of pessimism and the ice of cynicism, then and then only are you grown old—and then, indeed, as the ballad says, you just fade away.*

Perhaps it was the conception and pursuit of the positive ideal in whatever he did that kept MacArthur vigorous and productive throughout his life. MacArthur once said, "I promise to keep on living as though I expected to live forever," and with the exception of a few difficult periods in his life, he did seem to maintain a zest for life. He was never seriously ill until his early eighties, and he never retired in the accepted sense of the word. At 83, his last full year of life, he completed his memoirs; served as Chairman of the Board at Sperry Rand; and at President Kennedy's behest, successfully facilitated a settlement between the American Athletic Union and the National Collegiate Athletic Association, which were at an impasse regarding athletic eligibility for the upcoming Olympics.

Of course, MacArthur's idealism was not simply a strategy employed to stay young. It was a dynamic that informed many of the assignments he undertook in his career. In his approach to the revitalization of West Point in the early 1920s, MacArthur would not accept any assumed limitations. Instead, he began with an idealistic vision of what a West Point education could be. Then, as necessary, he adjusted and conformed his vision to the realities of the situation.

In the Japanese occupation, MacArthur pursued an idealized vision of what that defeated nation could become. That vision proved infectious to its citizens, who embraced many of the reforms aimed at democratizing their country. In September 1949, MacArthur wrote to an editor at the *Chicago Sun Times*:

> *Many skeptics behind the false facade of mythology, legend, and superstition have denied that this is possible, but experience demonstrates with unmistakable clarity that all any peoples need, be they of the East or West, the North or South, is the opportunity for greater individual liberty and higher personal dignity. Given this opportunity, no people on earth can fail to advance, for none hold a monopoly on human progress. This was the teaching of Jefferson in 1800. The lesson applies no less to Japan in 1949.*

Without a doubt, a solid sense of proportion is a necessary accompaniment to idealism. An idealistic vision that cannot be accomplished is a waste of resources and effort. But always question the veracity of limitations, and remember that because MacArthur began a task with an ambitious and idealistic vision, he maximized his results.

The vision that MacArthur presented of himself as a leader was as idealistic as the goals he set for himself. It is one reason why he became an iconic figure and a rallying point to millions of Americans, Filipinos, and Australians in WWII. His face was emblazoned on a wide range of products, such as calendars and coin banks. He was bombarded with requests for inspirational messages from labor unions and other groups. He invariably fulfilled these requests.

At the same time, MacArthur held himself to a high standard. He worked hard to live up to his image as an ideal leader. Whenever he was offered a share of the profits for the use of his image or name on products, for instance, MacArthur refused. "Appreciate greatly the distinction implied in your suggestion," he replied to one offer, "but feel that I cannot capitalize in any way the service I am honored to render my country."

"People grow old only by deserting their ideals."

Reflection Questions:

- Are you pursuing the highest standard of excellence in your leadership career?

- Is your organization pursuing a vision of perfection?

Chapter 39

Demonstrate Your Courage

Effective leadership requires courage. Leaders need courage to conceive and undertake personal and organizational risk, to accept accountability for failure, and to enlist followers in their cause. For all these reasons and more, MacArthur cultivated, demonstrated, and celebrated courage.

In the military, and in any other profession that carries the risk of bodily harm, physical courage becomes a vital concern. MacArthur articulated its importance on December 12, 1944, the day he presented the Medal of Honor to World War II flying ace Major Dick Bong. He said, "Of all military attributes that one which arouses the greatest admiration is courage. It is the basis of all successful military venture."

Even his critics agree that MacArthur's own physical courage was prodigious. There is not a single instance on record of him ever shirking danger. In WWI, during which he had field commands, he gained a fully merited reputation for fearlessness on the front lines. Even though a senior commander was never expected to expose himself to danger, MacArthur insisted on visiting combat zones during both WWII and the Korean War.

MacArthur received the Medal of Honor for his behavior on Corregidor, in which he was exposed to daily bombing raids for weeks on end. The Presidential citation accompanying the award begins to explain the leadership power inherent in courage:

> *His utter disregard of personal danger under heavy fire and aerial bombardment, his calm judgment in each crisis, inspired his troops, galvanized the spirit of resistance of the Filipino people, and confirmed the faith of the American people in their armed forces.*

Physical courage may not be a requirement in all organizations, but mental courage is always needed. Leaders need mental courage in pursuit of their own careers. MacArthur, for example, successfully faced a major test of his mental courage in his effort to gain admission to West Point.

Interestingly, although physical courage seemed a natural response to MacArthur, he sometimes had to work hard to maintain his mental courage. There were times in his life when the stakes were so critical that he had an extreme physical reaction to the stress. Thus, he was nauseated before the competitive test that earned him his appointment to the Academy. It is notable (and characteristic) that he invariably performed admirably in spite of his fear.

Leaders need mental courage to protect and secure the well-being of their organizations. During FDR's first term as president and MacArthur's tenure as Army Chief of Staff, the administration proposed huge cuts in military spending. MacArthur had the courage to argue with FDR over the cuts. He argued so vehemently that FDR reprimanded him. MacArthur apologized, but would not back down. In fact, he resigned on the spot. The budget cuts were reduced. Outside, the Secretary of War congratulated him. "But I just vomited on the steps of the White House," said MacArthur.

Leaders also need mental courage to support their organizational initiatives. MacArthur never shirked from putting his own career on the line for principles and strategies in which he believed. He did not always win, but his advocacy was often successful. The invasions of Luzon and Inchon are perfect examples of this point.

Finally, leaders must demonstrate their courage to establish their credibility, as well as motivate and influence their followers. This is clear in war, where battles have often been won when a leader steps forward and leads the charge. It is also true in more peaceful endeavors. MacArthur's entrance into Japan is a striking example of a leader establishing his credibility with a single act of courage.

Likewise, a lack of courage can have a critical effect on the morale and performance of followers. In WWII, MacArthur was undeservedly confronted with the negative impact that can result when a leader's courage is questioned. While he led the defense of the Philippines from Corregidor, the nickname "Dugout Doug" appeared among the troops on Bataan. They pictured their leader safe and well-fed while they were fighting on reduced rations, and the possibility of relief became less and less likely. This, of course, was not the real situation, but lampooning MacArthur was one of the few ways in which the troops could vent their frustration.

MacArthur never publicly responded to the nickname, which must have pained him greatly. Instead, he repeatedly proved it a fallacy through his actions. War correspondent William Dunn said: "Well, we used to have a saying during the war, 'If you want to be safe, stay close to the General. If you want to fly safely, get in the General's plane.' But you couldn't say that with MacArthur because he looked for it…he had absolutely no fear." MacArthur's courage was never questioned again. It is an important lesson: Leaders can't simply talk about courage; they must demonstrate it.

"[Courage] is the basis of all successful military venture."

Reflection Questions:

- What fears must you overcome to achieve your goals?

- How will you demonstrate your courage to your followers?

Chapter 40

Take Initiative

Great leaders act in anticipation of events, instead of in response to them, and they capture the advantages inherent in taking the first step. They are initiators. In war and peace, for better or for worse, MacArthur was an initiator, too. Like all effective leaders, he was willing to take the first step.

In light of his long military career, one of MacArthur's most interesting statements regarding initiative was aimed at a surprising goal, the abolition of war. After the development of nuclear weapons, he became convinced that the destructive capabilities of nations had rendered war obsolete. Thus, in a speech given in 1955, he said:

> *We must break out of the strait-jacket of the past. There must always be one to lead, and we should be that one. We should now proclaim our readiness to abolish war in concert with the great powers of the world. The result would be magical.*

MacArthur's willingness to be the one to lead, to take the initiative, was a constant throughout his career. When he found a problem, he did not simply report it; he sought to solve it. MacArthur's daring mission to locate railroad locomotives in Veracruz in 1914 is an early example of his initiative in action. Ironically, one reason why MacArthur, who was operating independently as a special agent for the Army's Chief of Staff, did not receive the Medal of Honor at that time was the fact that he undertook the mission without the knowledge of the local commanding officer in Veracruz.

When MacArthur spoke of the "magical" results that a peace initiative might have, he spoke from experience. The effects of his initiative changed world history. MacArthur's initiative was the driving force behind the Allied offensive in WWII's SW Pacific Theater. After the dismaying discovery that there was neither an army nor a grand strategy awaiting him in Australia, MacArthur refused to restrict his activities to building that nation's defenses. Instead, he peppered Army Chief of Staff George Marshall with requests for troops and materials. He used the media to put added pressure on Washington. MacArthur gained the support of Prime Minister John Curtin and the Australian nation, which provided troops and mobilized its industrial capacity to supply him with the majority of the resources he needed to get back into the fight. Without MacArthur's initiative, the war in the Pacific would have taken a radically different course.

No matter what orders MacArthur received, he always attempted to push them to their limits. MacArthur was also known to act first and seek approval later. On the first day of the Korean War, he dispatched a cargo ship of ammunition under air cover to the South Koreans and informed the Joint Chiefs of Staff afterward. Although the United States quickly committed itself to South Korea's defense, it was an act that predated that order and thus might have had enormous political ramifications.

Although MacArthur's initiative was often validated by subsequent events, initiative does have its proper limits. As President Truman's recall order demonstrates, all leaders have some constraints on their authority, and they must consider their actions in light of those restraints.

Further, a good leader uses initiative to attain goals, not to accumulate power and restrict the initiative of others. MacArthur understood that to delegate successfully and maximize organizational performance, a leader must have a staff that is empowered, willing, and able to take the initiative. His subordinates—men such as General George Kenney—not only appreciated this freedom, but drove themselves harder because of it.

When Kenney first came to Australia, the Air Force was in pitiful shape. The new air commander made an inspection tour and then told MacArthur that he wanted the autonomy to solve the personnel and equipment problems he had identified. MacArthur replied:

> *Go ahead. If you want to send someone home, you have my enthusiastic approval. As for your combat crews, you handle them. I don't care what they do, how they dress, or whether or not they salute, as long as they shoot down Jap planes and sink Jap ships. As for decorations, I'll give you the authority to award any medal except the Distinguished Service Cross…However, if one of your youngsters does something outstanding and you want to award him on the spot with D.S.C., go ahead and I'll approve it as soon as you tell me about it.*

Kenney quickly transformed the Air Force into an integral element in the drive back to the Philippines. "Yes," he later remembered, "it was fun to work for Douglas MacArthur."

"There must always be one to lead..."

Reflection Questions:

- Are you a proactive or reactive leader?

- Is everyone in your organization empowered to use their initiative?

Chapter 41

Prepare to Succeed

The need to prepare in anticipation of the future is not a new one. Twenty-six hundred years ago, a Greek slave named Aesop told the cautionary tale of an ant and a grasshopper. The ant collected food all summer; the grasshopper played and feasted. Which one was prepared for the inevitable coming of winter?

Leaders, too, must prepare. They must prepare for personal challenges that they will face in their lives and careers, and for the organizational challenges that they and their followers will face.

As a teenager, MacArthur became an early convert to the value of preparedness. He reaped the rewards of being well-prepared when he earned his appointment to West Point. "When the marks were counted, I led," he said. "My careful preparation had repaid me. It was lesson I never forgot. Preparedness is the key to success and victory."

MacArthur aggressively pursued personal preparedness during his education at West Point, and it is clear that that effort was a primary element in his excellent record as cadet. As a plebe, he shared quarters with an upperclassman, so he had an additional hour before lights-out. MacArthur used that time for extra study and also often rose an hour before reveille for extra study time. A fellow cadet named Julian Schley later said, "MacArthur studied harder than any other member of the class. He was a brilliant man, but he didn't lean on it."

Preparedness also became a watchword in MacArthur's many leadership roles. One of his notable victories as superintendent of West Point was the reinstatement of a four-year course of education. The Academy's program had been drastically shortened to one year during WWI, but it did not return immediately to the full four years after the war. Instead, in 1919, it was expanded to only three years. MacArthur knew that four full years were needed to prepare and educate new officers, so he prepared a proposal and rallied support for that term. In early 1920, he testified during the ensuing Congressional hearings and the full four-year program was re-established.

In 1942, when MacArthur was desperately scrounging up all the manpower he could muster in the southwest Pacific, the current superintendent of West Point asked for his opinion on the issue of reducing the educational program to more quickly graduate officers. MacArthur's reply was brusque: "I am unalterably opposed to shortening the course of instruction at West Point. The disastrous results of such a policy were clearly demonstrated during the last war."

As Chief of Staff in the 1930s, MacArthur, in his quest of military preparedness, was savaged by critics who characterized him as "an insatiable pillager of the public purse" and a "thief." Yet, years before the attack on Pearl Harbor, when the need became obvious to all, he called for the stockpiling of raw materials essential for military production. It was also his idea to award small initial orders to those industrial firms that would in the future be called upon to supply new types of military goods to the Army. MacArthur reasoned that these "educational orders" would ensure rapid mobilization in case of attack. The companies would use the small orders to gain the knowledge and create the equipment and methods needed to produce the goods. If and when the goods were needed in large quantities, they would be prepared and able to quickly attain maximum production levels.

The theme of preparedness and its value as a deterrent to war is a constant in MacArthur's speeches and writings during those years. In 1935, at the annual gathering of Rainbow Division veterans, he said, "Every nation that would preserve its tranquility, its riches, its independence, and its self-respect must keep alive its martial ardor and be at all times prepared to defend itself." He looked back through history at all of the nations that had fallen "through degeneracy of military capacity because of unpreparedness," and concluded: "Let us be prepared, lest we, too, perish."

Two decades later, in his testimony in the Congressional hearings that followed his recall from Korea in 1951, MacArthur provided a rationale for preparedness that should still ring true to military, political, and business leaders more than 50 years later:

> *You know the acuteness of modern war is increasing very vividly. It took a long time in the old days before the war machines really began to roll. But with integration of the world, [and] increase in scientific methods of destruction, the blow falls much quicker; that is, you don't get the time now to prepare that you had in the past...[and] with every passing year that diminishes.*

Many leaders would prefer to be seen as grasshoppers, nimbly leaping from one victory to another, than plodding ants—and MacArthur was no exception. The innovative island-hopping campaigns between Papua and the Philippines gave rise to the legend of MacArthur as an intuitive genius. What was not emphasized, however, was the long preparation that preceded the conception and execution of these battles. MacArthur won his victories and enjoyed the reputation that inevitably followed because he prepared himself and his forces as thoroughly as possible.

"Preparedness is the key to success and victory."

Reflection Questions:

- What preparations can you undertake today in order to achieve the next level in your career?

- What skills and knowledge does your organization need in order to meet tomorrow's challenges?

Chapter 42

Learn Continuously

Learning is an essential ingredient in preparedness. It is also a lifelong pursuit. Leaders prepare themselves and their organizations for success by embracing and enhancing their ability to learn.

MacArthur was one of the lucky ones. The love of learning caught fire within him while he was still a schoolboy. He quite eloquently described the transformation it engendered in his attitude toward his studies:

> *There came a desire to know, a seeking for the reason why, a search for the truth. Abstruse mathematics began to appear as a challenge to analysis, dull Latin and Greek seemed a gateway to the moving words of leaders of the past, laborious historical data led to the nerve-tingling battlefields of the great captains, Biblical lessons began to open spiritual portals of a growing faith, literature to lay bare the souls of men.*

Three-quarters of a century later, just a few months before his death, MacArthur reiterated the importance of learning to a delegation of cadets visiting from West Point. He spoke of the need to rely on intelligence, rather than sentiment or emotion. "Sentimentalism has muddied many problems, has settled none. Intellect is a man's only hope for improvement over his present state." Intellect is our capacity to learn and understand.

Continuous attention to the building of a leader's intellect means that learning must entail more than formal schooling. Like so many great leaders, MacArthur was a voracious reader who consumed up to three books a day, in addition to newspapers and magazines. General Charles West, who served in Tokyo headquarters, said, "The man was the fastest reader I've ever known in my life. I've seen him go through a document a half-inch thick. This is a sort of legend...you'd hear about MacArthur but couldn't believe, but weeks later he would quote whole paragraphs from that document that he just rippled through as I watched him."

MacArthur appears to have gained his habit of reading from his family. While stationed in the Philippines, his father had a standing order with a Hong Kong bookseller for all books regarding Far Eastern affairs. MacArthur inherited his father's library, which had grown to 7,000 to 8,000 volumes when the bulk of it was lost in Japan's invasion of the Philippines. By his death in 1964, MacArthur had rebuilt it to 5,000 volumes. It remains intact and on display in the archive building of the MacArthur Memorial in Norfolk, VA.

How well we learn depends on our ability to elicit and comprehend information. Although MacArthur's ability to dominate a meeting with a lengthy and highly articulate exposition is more often noted, the record shows that he was also an acute listener. In fact, when he believed that he could learn from a conversation, it was his habit to listen first and refrain from speaking as much as possible. He was also a master questioner.

William Ganoe, MacArthur's chief of staff at West Point, described their first meeting like this:

> *...[MacArthur] caught sight of my letter of resignation.*
>
> *"Well, what's this?" he asked, touching it at arm's length and pushing it away without the faintest attempt to pick it up and read it. Before I could answer, he shot out a question about a condition on the reservation. As I answered, another came so fast I could hardly collect myself. Then they accelerated so much that they overlapped my answers. By the light of his eye, I could see he understood before I had finished.*
>
> *The rapid-fire quiz kept on. He went from the South Gate to Popolopen, from the Cavalry Detachment to the Commissary, from the Officers' Club to the Observatory, from the Commandant to the Cadet Store. Where had he got his information for the intelligence behind the questions? They gathered force as they went on without grunts or hems like a record player working up to a climax. He was as sure of what he wanted to know as he was of seeing me. I pressed and was pressed so hard, I sometimes stumbled. Yet there was nothing of the severe or inquisitorial about his manner, no show of passion or hounding. It was smooth and almost casual as if he were asking my opinion of a play. But it was clipped and persistent.*

Broad-based learning, often the most valuable source of innovation, requires exposure to a wide range of information sources. As West Point's superintendent, MacArthur sought to expose cadets to diverse and international views. He invited scholars, leaders, and experts—including the Prince of Wales, France's Marshal Ferdinand Foch, and airman Billy Mitchell—to visit West Point and address the Cadet Corps. He also made contemporary affairs a part of the curriculum by insisting that the reading of two newspapers daily be added to classes in history and government.

As superintendent, MacArthur also added the practical experience of living to the previously cloistered existence of cadets. He liberalized social and leave policies, hoping to create a "means of keeping in touch with life outside the walls of the institution" and graduate officers who had more experience than "a high school boy."

"Intellect is a man's only hope for improvement over his present state."

Reflection Questions:

- Do you have time set aside for learning about subjects both within and beyond your field of expertise?

- How are you encouraging your followers to expand their own intellects?

Chapter 43

Study History

While the Internet boom was driving the irrationally exuberant financial markets at the turn of the millennium, many business leaders and investors believed that a breakpoint in economic history had occurred, that historical measures of performance were irrelevant. They paid a steep price for ignoring history when the boom turned to bust. When it comes to history, past performance is a relevant indicator of future success. That is why savvy leaders study history.

Even a superficial browse through his personal library makes it clear that MacArthur read deeply in the subject of history. Indeed, he was a committed student of history. In 1963, when Columbia University was considering the establishment of a chair in international history in MacArthur's honor, he said:

> *If there is one thing I have learned during my long years of experience, it is that if we would correctly solve the problems of the present and chart a safe course into the future we must study and weigh and understand the manifold lessons of which history is the great—indeed the only—competent teacher. For as Cicero put it 80 years before the birth of Christ, "Not to know what happened before one was born is always to be a child."*

In August 1941, at a time when the Nazi war machine appeared unstoppable, correspondent William Dunn was surprised to hear MacArthur predict the outcome of Hitler's thus far highly successful

Russia campaign and then his ultimate defeat. "This marks the beginning of the end for Adolf Hitler," MacArthur flatly declared. This was the first positive comment Dunn had heard, and he replied that many observers were expecting a total Russian collapse. MacArthur responded:

> *They haven't studied their history. Napoleon made the same mistake, and Hitler will wind up just as Bonaparte did, and with infinitely greater losses. The Russians will never surrender. They have unlimited manpower, and they can retreat, mile by mile, clear across Siberia. In two months the rains will start, and a month later the Russian winter will set in. No people in the world can withstand a Russian winter like the Russians, certainly not the Germans.*

Two months later, as it became clear that the Germans had bogged down in Russia, MacArthur told Dunn, "History, Bill, just history! It was all there, but Hitler didn't read it, or else he didn't believe it."

MacArthur applied the lessons of history to assist him in understanding the causes of events and to analyze potential responses. He was, said General Edward Almond (a corps commander under MacArthur in Korea) "a master of historical analogy...a constant searcher for the motive of the proposition at hand; and he reasoned, not from the statement of the motive, but from the historical background of the people whose country he was dealing with."

MacArthur's own advice regarding the best uses of history is worth considering:

> *But the military student does not seek to learn from history the minutiae of method and technic. In every age these are decisively influenced by the characteristics of weapons currently available and by the means at hand for maneuvering, supplying, and controlling combat forces. But research does bring to light those fundamental principles and their combinations and applications, which, in the past, have been productive of success. These principles know no limitations of time.*

MacArthur's belief in history's timeless principles explains how Genghis Khan came to be featured in the 1935 annual report of the Army Chief of Staff. MacArthur focused his report on the creation of a highly mobile Army capable of fast response. To illustrate the soundness of his thesis, he reached back 700 years to one of history's most successful armies:

[Genghis Khan] insisted upon speed in action, a speed which by comparison with other forces of his day was almost unbelievable. Though he armed his men with the best equipment of offense and defense that the skill of Asia could produce, he refused to encumber them with loads that would immobilize his army. Over great distances his legions moved so rapidly and secretly as to astound his enemies and practically paralyze their powers of resistance. He crossed great rivers and mountain ranges, he reduced walled cities in his path, and swept onward to destroy nations and pulverize whole civilizations. On the battlefield his troops maneuvered so swiftly and skillfully and struck with such devastating speed that times without number they defeated armies overwhelmingly superior to themselves in numbers.

Regardless of his destructiveness, his cruelty, his savagery, he clearly understood the unvarying necessities of war... We cannot violate these laws and still produce and sustain the kind of army that alone can ensure the integrity of our country and the permanency of our institutions if ever again we face the grim realities of war.

"...history is the great—indeed the only—competent teacher."

Reflection Questions:

- Are there historical figures who faced and successfully navigated events that mirror your current situation?

- What are the principles behind their solutions, and how can you apply them today?

Chapter 44

Exude Confidence

Confidence is a vital leadership trait. Leaders must believe in themselves, their organizations, and the achievement of their stated goals. Confidence is the mechanism by which they exhibit their conviction in those beliefs.

MacArthur had such a well-developed sense of confidence that he was often mistakenly characterized as egomaniacal. But MacArthur did not fit the definition: He was not obsessively preoccupied with himself. Instead, he was expert at the application of the confidence that derives from a healthy ego to the achievement of his goals.

Leaders first require self-confidence, which is the internal confidence that supports their ability to point the way, stand by their decisions, and pursue their goals. It becomes particularly important in the face of the dissent and criticism that occurs when leaders break new ground.

"Scoffers will never be lacking when any new concept is advanced," MacArthur said. "Usually, however, they are found among those who know little or nothing of the facts, but who arrogate to themselves the dogmatic wisdom of popular slogan and glib generality." As usual, he reached back into history to support his point:

> *Let me remind you that there were a multitude of skeptics who maintained that Fulton's steamboat would not float, that the Arnacal flight would not reach Madrid, that the Wright brothers would not get their airplane off the ground, that Ericsson's Monitor would be a dismal failure, and that Marconi was a visionary at best, and possibly a lunatic at the worst. Defeatists have always been present to greet every new thought, every new idea, and every new attempt at constructive progress. Defeatists laughed at America's attempt to free herself from British control, but today the United States is possibly the most powerful nation in the world.*

Leaders must exhibit confidence to gain support. Followers look to their leaders for cues, and if they don't perceive confidence, they often hesitate to commit their full energy and resources to the task at hand. As an observer of MacArthur once asked, "How would you like to go into battle behind a general with an inferiority complex?"

MacArthur was fully aware of the advantages that confidence can engender. He used his self-confidence to sell his strategies, to bolster the morale of troops, and to establish his own authority. MacArthur also valued confidence in the officers who reported to him. Among the criteria he expected of the field officers under his command was "that demeanor of confidence, self-reliance, and assurance which is the birthright of all cultured gentlemen and the special trademark of the Army officer."

Of course, confidence alone does not make a leader. Unwarranted confidence is dangerous, particularly in war. By and large, MacArthur avoided this trap. William Dunn offered a good description of the qualities that support confidence, when he said that MacArthur's self-confidence was "...a reasonable characteristic in a man whose belief in himself was based on a sound education; long years of experience; a thorough knowledge of the military science that had dominated his life; and, extremely important at that time, an almost uncanny understanding of the enemy he was fighting."

Finally, leaders must protect and replenish their stores of confidence. Although MacArthur is often portrayed as an imperious detached figure, he was, like almost all people, sensitive to criticism. Those who knew him intimately agree that he was often hurt by the many attacks he attracted during his career.

One way MacArthur protected his confidence was to reframe criticism as a sign of progress. When he was under heavy fire at West Point, he told his Chief of Staff, "Proves we are right. If there were no dissenters, we wouldn't be accomplishing anything. It's only with retchings that a noble institution gives up a bad habit."

MacArthur also looked to his heroes for support. He possessed a quote from Abraham Lincoln that was hung in his Tokyo office. It read:

> *If I were to try to read, much less answer, all the attacks made on me, this shop might as well be closed for any other business. I do the very best I know how, the very best I can, and I mean to keep doing so until the end. If the end brings me out all right, what is said against me won't amount to anything. If the end brings me out wrong, ten thousand angels swearing I was right would make no difference.*

"Scoffers will never be lacking."

Reflection Questions:

- How can you bolster self-confidence in your capabilities and decisions?

- Does a sense of confidence pervade your organization?

Chapter 45

Get the Athletic Advantage

Both leaders and their organizations need to be physically healthy if they expect to perform at peak levels. Robust health supports the drive to success in two ways: It ensures that we are physically able to perform and that our cognitive functions receive the proper care and feeding.

Leaders are always in motion. They work hard, often keeping torturous schedules and logging many hours of travel. They also think hard, applying their intellects to the complex challenges they and their organizations must undertake. To maintain their efforts and ensure peak performance, they hone their bodies as well as their minds.

MacArthur's physical fitness enabled him to enjoy what were essentially two careers. In 1941, as WWII loomed and MacArthur was called back to active duty by President Roosevelt, he had already completed a full career that had stretched from his education as cadet to the highest leadership position in the Army. Yet, his most notable achievements still lay before him. From age 61 until his death at age 84, at a time when most of his contemporaries were long retired, MacArthur undertook an even more demanding second career that included command roles in the Pacific War, occupied Japan, and the Korean War.

Physical fitness played an important enabling role in the longevity of MacArthur's career. He was healthy throughout almost all his adult life. He kept very long hours, but he also typically stopped for a long lunch and an afternoon nap. MacArthur ate well and sparingly. He had a daily routine of calisthenics that he continued into his sixties. He was a walker; all day, he paced up and down his office as he worked out problems and conducted meetings. Staff physician Roger Egeberg once calculated that MacArthur walked "at least five miles per day and at about three miles per hour."

MacArthur understood the important role that fitness plays in leadership, particularly in the often physically demanding life of a military officer. This became the rationale behind his lifelong support of athletics.

When MacArthur expanded the physical fitness programs and required cadets to participate in intramural athletics at West Point, he was remembering the condition of (and the demands made on) the infantrymen of WWI. "Troops in poor physical condition are worthless," he flatly stated.

Further, MacArthur saw athletics as a useful organizational development tool. Team sports teach teamwork; they teach aggressive competitiveness within a framework of fair play. In 1922, he reported from West Point:

> *Nothing more quickly than competitive athletics brings out the qualities of leadership, quickness of decision, promptness of action, mental and muscular coordination, aggressiveness, and courage. And nothing so readily and so firmly establishes that indefinable spirit of group interest and pride which we know as morale. The cadets graduated under this system will be not only the most efficient leaders themselves, but will be equipped for supervising athletics and giving practical instruction therein to the men of their organizations.*

Team sports also teach leaders and their followers how to execute under pressure. General Alexander Haig explained:

> *It was General MacArthur who convinced me that the tensions on the athletic field were the only peacetime activities that compared to the kinds of tensions which you face on the battlefield. That's why he was a great advocate of athletics in the training of professional soldiers. Fighting in sports, in war, or in business challenges your ability to integrate human efforts under tension.*

At the same time, athletics provide a means to relieve pressure. They are a form of play. MacArthur enjoyed the playing field. He treasured the varsity letter he earned for playing left field on West Point's baseball team. In his eighties, it adorned his bathrobe.

MacArthur was also an avid fan of athletics. He closely followed West Point football throughout his life. In December 1944, while MacArthur was in the midst of planning the Luzon campaign in the Philippines, West Point beat Navy in the last game of a perfect season and won its first national championship. He cabled head coach Earl "Red" Blaik: "The greatest of all Army teams. We have stopped the war to celebrate your magnificent success." In the late 1940s, when Vince Lombardi coached at West Point, he would telephone MacArthur on Saturday mornings to discuss game strategy.

When MacArthur served as Army Chief of Staff, he was instrumental in the approval of a major expansion of West Point's facilities. His words were carved into the stone over the entrance to the new gymnasium:

Upon the fields of friendly strife
Are sown the seeds
That, upon other fields, on other days
Will bear the fruits of victory

"We must build athletically not only for health but for character. In learning how to play we learn how to live."

Reflection Questions:

- Do you devote at least one half-hour per day to physical exercise?

- What athletic and fitness activities does your organization offer to employees?

Chapter 46

Master the Art of Communication

The most influential method of communication that a leader has at his disposal is his voice. A leader's voice is not solely a vocal instrument; it encompasses communication via the written word and via symbolic gestures. Great leaders are experts in each of these modes of communication.

One of MacArthur's most remarked-on traits was his mastery of the art of communication. He took full advantage of his communication skills, but he rarely talked about them. One of the few statements on record is a 1939 letter in response to a West Point professor's query about the proper objectives of the Academy's English program. MacArthur replied:

> *It is unquestionably so to train the cadet that he can clearly and lucidly present his basic thoughts and ideas. It is not the mission of the English Course to create or control those ideas, but it is its clear function to provide him with the medium through which he can present his views in an intelligent and even forcible manner. No man can hope to rise to distinction who cannot do this and no man, however humble his position, should fail to be able to do so. It is the very medium in which modern civilization lives. It is almost like the air you breathe. Without it, a man may have the finest judgment in the world, he may be even wise as Solomon, and yet his influence will be practically negligible. The accomplishment of such a purpose is not confined to proper grammatical, rhetorical, or phonetical grouping of words into sentences and paragraphs. There must be the logical connection between the thought in a man's brain and the ability to present it in clear language.*

MacArthur's command of the spoken word was complete, and his oratory (a gift that seems to have been a birthright) failed on only rare occasions. A fellow cadet at West Point said: "In the classroom, [MacArthur] put on a wonderful show. Whenever he had a recitation to make, it was a finished product. He had a commanding presence. He talked well and he usually knew his stuff. Whenever he didn't know his stuff, it was pretty hard to tell if he did or didn't, and he usually got away with it."

President Dwight Eisenhower, a five-star general himself, noted MacArthur's ability to speak on informal social occasions: "He was a captivating, spell-binding talker at social functions. I remember a dinner in Manila after which he kept a large group of guests in rapt attention for hours with his monologue, talking with gestures and feeling and intimate knowledge of many topics far afield of military matters."

Although MacArthur liked to use advanced and archaic vocabulary, one reason for his skill at "spell-binding" was the clarity with which he spoke. General Lewis Brereton, who served under MacArthur as the head of the Far East Air Force in the Philippines, said, "There is never any doubt as to what he means and what he wants."

Another reason for MacArthur's effectiveness as a speaker was his physical delivery. His voice, pacing, and physical gestures became part of a performance. *Time-Life* reporter Richard Lauterbach elaborates:

> *Emphasizing a point, he would spring out of his chair, reach his desk in two giant steps, pick up a box of matches, and rattle them over his head like a saber. With head reared back and chin jutting out, he would begin answering, and the words rolled forth as if they were heaven's final dictum on the subject. For emphasis, MacArthur employed a sort of breathless eloquence, almost whispering a word here, drawing out a word there, then clipping one very short.*

MacArthur's written skills were also highly developed. Like most high-ranking leaders, he did have writers working for him. But he put his imprimatur on his communications by always playing an active role in their preparation. His wife Jean remembers him composing the "Old Soldiers" speech for Congress over a six- to eight-hour period on the plane trip back from Japan. The draft of his memoirs, which were published shortly after his death, is in the archives of the MacArthur Memorial. He wrote by hand on lined pads. His sentences are complete, and there is little revision.

Finally, MacArthur understood the power and use of symbols. One way in which he kept his promise to return to the Philippines alive was through constant symbolic reminders. The plane in which he traveled was emblazoned with the name *Bataan*, as was the telephone exchange for his headquarters in Australia. When a delegation of Japanese officials flew to the Philippines to make arrangements for the surrender and requested call letters for their plane, MacArthur's answer was clear, as usual: "Tell them they will use the letters B-A-T-A-A-N."

"There must be the logical connection between the thought in a man's brain and the ability to present it in clear language."

Reflection Questions:

- How can you use symbols to reiterate and reinforce your messages and goals?

- Does your organization's development programs include communication skills training?

Chapter 47

Forge Emotional Bonds

Leaders build emotional connections between people. To be successful, they must connect stakeholders into cohesive groups—in business, for instance, these groups include employees, customers, and communities. They also build connections between various constituencies so that different groups can effectively work together. In other words, leaders forge the emotional bonds that hold groups together and enable them to perform.

MacArthur first demonstrated his ability to create emotional connections with soldiers. In his first command at Fort Leavenworth, he transformed the worst company on the post to one of the best. Later, as Chief of Staff of the Rainbow Division, he was responsible for melding National Guard units from 26 different states into an effective fighting force. The resulting bonds, strengthened by their experiences in WWI, became lifelong connections between the division's soldiers.

MacArthur went on to undertake much greater challenges in bond-building. He brought together the allied fighting forces of different nations in WWII and Korea. In the occupation of Japan, he successfully undertook the greatest challenge of all: creating positive and enduring connections between bitter enemies.

Empathy, the ability to understand the situation and psychology of others, is a key quality in the forging of emotional bonds. Whether it was in dealing with members of his immediate staff or with millions of foreign nationals, MacArthur always sought to understand the thinking and the motivations behind their actions.

MacArthur used empathetic reasoning to guide his actions. Perhaps it was egotistical to declare, "I shall return" instead of "We shall return," but MacArthur knew that the Filipino people did not have overly positive bonds with the United States and felt abandoned by Washington. In contrast, MacArthur not only had strong ties to the archipelago that stretched back to his father's time, but he had also been their military leader until WWII. He understood that his personal promise would more effectively bolster Filipino morale and resistance.

Empathy also tempers a leader's perceptions of others and enables positive interactions. One positive experience leads to another, and everyone benefits. A positive cycle of reinforcement similar to this can be seen in the early years of the Japanese Occupation, and it had its genesis in MacArthur's treatment of the Japanese.

The Pacific War was a bitter one, in which many people on both sides thought of their opponents as subhuman. MacArthur never succumbed to the race hatred that was engendered by the war. Charles West, who was with MacArthur during the war and in Tokyo in the first year of the occupation, said, "I never heard General MacArthur say one derogatory thing about the Japanese. He respected them as a people, and he realized how important they were as a nation in the world and in our strategic scheme of things in the years to come."

MacArthur, in 1930, defined this empathic understanding and treatment as a "principle of conduct" in the peaceful and productive merging of the eastern and western nations. He said:

> *The first is tolerance. History teaches us that when two races are brought by the working of an inscrutable Providence to live together, tolerance, a sympathetic understanding of each other's desires, hopes and aspirations, is the inescapable necessity. It is a quality in the exercise of which both sides find honor. It raises to sublimity him who extends it, and him who by accepting it, shows his readiness to return it in kind.*

Empathy also enables compassion, an important trait that sometimes appears to be in short supply among leaders. Compassionate leaders not only seek to understand and sympathize with the problems of their constituents, but they also actively help solve those problems.

MacArthur displayed a striking ability to open himself up to the problems and suffering of others. He was particularly concerned with the fate of those held in the Japanese prison camps during the liberation of the Philippines. MacArthur decorated every participant in the daring raid on Cabanatuan, which in late January 1945 rescued the 400 Bataan veterans imprisoned there. He personally awarded Distinguished Service Crosses to the raid's two leaders, saying, "[N]othing in this entire campaign has given me so much personal satisfaction."

Dr. Ralph Hibbs, who was rescued in the raid, remembered MacArthur's emotional visit to the field hospital where the Cabanatuan prisoners were treated. MacArthur apologized for taking so long to free them and he cried. "I wondered whether the general's visit was a guilt trip," Hibbs said, "but his grief could not have been more genuine."

"...tolerance, a sympathetic understanding of each other's desires, hopes, and aspirations, is the inescapable necessity."

Reflection Questions:

- How can you build your empathy for the least-understood stake-holder group in your organization?

- How can you communicate your respect and compassion for your followers?

Chapter 48

Develop Your Media Savvy

Today's world is connected by a vast media network. Sound bytes and images flash around the globe 24/7. Anyone with Internet access can read a dozen stories on a newsworthy—or not-so-newsworthy—event within minutes of its occurrence. In this world, the attention of the media is a two-edged sword that leaders need to handle with great care.

MacArthur was one of the 20th century's most media-savvy leaders. To be sure, he experienced both edges of the media sword, but he also clearly understood how to utilize the power of the media to achieve his goals.

MacArthur was introduced to the ways of the media in 1916, when he was given charge of the War Department's newly established Bureau of Information. He was, in essence, the Army's first PR man and as such, he learned how to write press releases, influence reporters, and control interviews.

In this position, MacArthur was instrumental in the public acceptance of the Selective Service Act of 1917, the potentially explosive legislation that for the first time gave the President the right to draft citizens. In that same year, the concept for the Rainbow Division was borne of MacArthur's flair for PR. In response to the problem of which state's

National Guard would be the first to be called to war, MacArthur suggested a multistate division "that will stretch over the whole country like a rainbow."

MacArthur was also extremely successful at establishing cooperative relations with the press during his tenure at the Board of Information. In a unique occurrence in the annals of press relations, all 29 members of the War Department press corps sent a letter of commendation for his services to the Secretary of War. They wrote:

> *We feel no doubt of what the future holds for Major MacArthur. Rank and honors will come to him if merit can bring them to any man; but we now wish to say our thanks to him for the unfailing kindness, patience, and wise counsel we have received from him in the difficult days that are past.*
>
> *Our needs have compelled us to tax that patience at all hours of the day and night. We have never failed to receive courteous treatment from him. Although the censorship imposed was but a voluntary obligation upon the press, it has been kept faithfully, and we feel that is has been largely because of the fair, wise, and liberal way in which Major MacArthur exercised his functions that this was possible. He has put his own personality into his task.*

MacArthur's positions provided access to the highest levels of media, and he ensured that access by creating and nurturing an enviable network of contacts. His network included journalists (such as Hugh Baillie, the head of United Press, and Roy Howard, head of Scripps-Howard) and publishers (including William Randolph Hearst, Robert McCormick, and Henry Luce).

MacArthur skillfully used his position and his platform with the media to elicit support for his objectives and to pressure his superiors into providing the resources to achieve them. When he finally reached Melbourne in 1942, he stepped from the train and immediately put the media to work on his behalf with a short public statement that concluded:

> *No general can make something out of nothing. My success or failure will depend primarily upon the resources which the respective governments place at my disposal. My faith in them is complete. In any event I shall do my best. I shall keep the soldier's faith.*

MacArthur's WWII press releases, known as communiqués, have often been criticized for self-aggrandizement and exaggeration. Paul Rogers, who worked closely with MacArthur and his Chief of Staff Richard Sutherland, said, "Most critics failed to understand that MacArthur did not write the communiqué for the benefit of his troops, the press, or the politicians in Canberra, London, and Washington...He wrote his communiqué to focus the attention of the American people on [the southwest Pacific theater] and its needs."

These public releases might also have been used to confuse the enemy. General Frederick Munson, who also served in MacArthur's headquarters in WWII, said: "General MacArthur would confuse the Japanese by sending out communiqués...They didn't know what to think. I think it was just sheer brilliance."

As for MacArthur's own advice on how to deal with aggressive and provocative reporters, this is what his pilot Weldon "Dusty" Rhodes heard him say:

> *I learned the hard way that in handling the press if you ignore their statements there's nothing they can do. They will label you as uncooperative, but there's no comeback that they can have. On the other hand, if you argue with them, they keep it going batting the ball back and forth in their own way and they finally control what they finally say. So, just don't get in an argument with the press.*

"I am working very hard with my newspapermen."

Reflection Questions:

- Have you completed media relations training with a professional?

- What media-worthy activities are currently occurring in your organization?

Chapter 49

Embrace Innovation

Innovation is the lifeblood of all organizations. It represents the ways and means of improving what already exists and the leaps of creativity that enable breakthroughs into new, uncharted territory. Organizations need innovation to survive and prosper. Leaders provide the encouragement and impetus that the innovative spirit needs to thrive.

Between his birth in 1880 and the end of WWI in 1919, MacArthur lived in a world that was as thoroughly transformed by innovation as our world has been in recent years. Electric lights, motor vehicles, moving pictures and radio, the airplane—all these things and more emerged in the first half of his life. Perhaps because he lived in a world driven by technological breakthroughs and change, he developed a keen awareness that a static organization was a dying one.

As a military leader, MacArthur preached the need for innovation. In 1931, as Chief of Staff, he gave a radio address prior to a nationwide exercise demonstrating the capabilities of the growing U.S Army Air Force. It was a compelling statement on the power of innovation:

> *Wars are largely won through new ideas and inventions. The great captains of history have all been innovators. They have had background, but they have not looked backward.*

The military tabulations of the world's battlefields read like an index of new weapons, new equipment, new conceptions which have in result swayed the destinies of mankind. War chariots, elephants, the Roman sword, chain-mail, gunpowder, the bayonet, the ramrod, permanent regular formations as devised by the Ottoman Turks, the regimenting of religious enthusiasm by Mohammed, the railroad, the telegraphy, the airplane, the General Staff—each in its turn has brought victory.

A sure indication of health and virility in military thought is to refuse to be bound down by the limitations of equipment at present in use. We must hold our minds alert and receptive not only to the six-mile ceiling bomber and the mile-a-minute combat car which are already on the military horizon, but to the application of unglimpsed methods and weapons that the engineer, the chemist, and the physicist may provide. The next war will be won in the future, not in the past. We must go on, or we will go under.

Innovation played an important role in the triphibious strategy that MacArthur adopted in the island campaigns in the SW Pacific. The PT boat, for instance, became a fixture in the Pacific at MacArthur's urging. In the late 1930s, he envisioned a Philippines "navy" of small torpedo boats that could maneuver in tight spaces and shallow waters and would "have distinct effect in compelling any hostile force to approach cautiously and by small detachments." Only a few "Q-boats" were built before the war, but they became the model on which the PT boat was based.

Rapid innovation in air force methods and equipment enabled the highly successful "hit 'em where they ain't" strategy. Air commander George Kenney became a favorite of MacArthur because of his willingness to innovate. The development of parachute fragmentation bombs and the refinement of skip-bombing techniques increased the effectiveness of the bombers in the Pacific. The installation of extra gas tanks gave fighters added range and were instrumental in MacArthur's successful 550-mile leap to Hollandia and the virtually total destruction of the enemy air power that the Japanese believed was safely amassed there.

At age 82, MacArthur was still imagining the ramifications of innovation, for better and for worse. In 1962, echoing President Kennedy's "New Frontier" theme, he told the cadets of West Point:

We are reaching out for a new and boundless frontier. We speak in strange terms: of harnessing the cosmic energy; of making winds and tides work for us; of creating unheard-of synthetic materials to supplement and even replace our old standard basics; of purifying sea water for our drink; of mining ocean floors for new fields of wealth and food; of disease preventatives to expand life into the hundreds of years; of controlling the weather for a more equitable distribution of heat and cold, of rain and shine; of spaceships to the moon; of the primary target in war no longer limited to the armed forces of an enemy, but instead to include his civilian population; of ultimate conflict between a united human race and the sinister forces of some other planetary galaxy; of such dreams and fantasies as to make life the most exciting of all times.

"The great captains of history have all been innovators."

Reflection Questions:

- What is your natural response to new ideas and technologies; how can you increase your openness to and acceptance of innovation?

- How can you encourage and enhance your organization's receptiveness to innovation?

Chapter 50

Accept Risk

Many leaders eschew risk. They perceive it in a negative light and struggle to avoid it. But in Portugal in the 16th century, the word "risk" was used to describe the great sea voyages of exploration, and one of its root meanings was "to dare."

Although MacArthur approached risk as a daring venture, he was not foolhardy when it came to risk. He understood that there is risk in every alternative, including that alternative of *not* acting; and he carefully weighed, minimized, and managed the risks that he undertook.

The invasion of Los Negros in the Admiralty Islands, which secured a fleet anchorage and provided a key point in the isolation of the Japanese stronghold at Rabaul, is a striking example of MacArthur's approach to risk. The invasion was originally planned for March 1944, but when reconnaissance revealed a dearth of enemy activity, MacArthur made a fast decision to capture it a month earlier than planned (and with only 1,000 troops in the 1st Cavalry Brigade instead of a full division).

MacArthur's staff opposed the operation. It allowed them only four days to mount the invasion, and in light of previous estimates (which turned out to be accurate) of 4,000 Japanese troops on the island, they believed that the invasion force could be easily overwhelmed on the beach. MacArthur overruled them. Based on previous behavior of the Japanese,

MacArthur was convinced that they would not mount a major defense on the beach with their full force and that the surprise attack would succeed.

The risk paid off. The 1st Cavalry Brigade took and held the beach, the Japanese never mounted a concerted attack, and the Admiralty Islands were captured by mid-March. The jump to Los Negros enabled MacArthur to eliminate three previously planned operations, with the attendant savings in lives and resources; Rabaul was cut off sooner than had been planned; and the great leap to Hollandia was enabled.

Of course, risk-taking is not always so rewarding, and some failures are inevitable. But Los Negros was a carefully calculated bet on MacArthur's part. Just prior to the invasion, General Courtney Whitney recalled that one of MacArthur's commanders again suggested the operation's cancellation, calling it a "gamble with the deck of cards in the enemy's hands as dealer." MacArthur replied, "Yes, but a gamble in which I have everything to win; little to lose. I bet ten to win a million if I hit the jackpot."

MacArthur hedged his bet on Los Negros in two ways. First, he purposely placed only a relatively small force at risk. Reinforcements were held until the outcome of the landing was determined. Second, he personally accompanied the invading force. It was another example of the "reconnaissance in force" concept, in which MacArthur minimized the risk of flaws in his strategy by being on the scene to make immediate adjustments if necessary.

MacArthur did hit the jackpot on Los Negros, but he was well aware that the risks he took could easily have turned out differently. In his successful evacuation from the Philippines to Australia, the PT boats that took MacArthur, his family, and his staff on the first leg of the journey had to run the enemy blockade of Manila. The Japanese heard the boat's motors and barely missed locating and intercepting it on several occasions.

On MacArthur's arrival at Cagayan on the Philippines island of Mindanao, his party boarded planes for the final leg of the trip to Australia. This time, they had to divert from their intended landing point at Darwin because of an enemy air raid. When the party finally landed safely at Batchelor Field, the report of approaching enemy aircraft forced them to leave immediately for Alice Springs in the center of the continent. After their arrival, MacArthur told his chief of staff Richard Sutherland, "It was close, but that's the way it is in war. You win or lose, live or die—and the difference is just an eyelash."

MacArthur had a long record of successful risk taking, but like every leader, he did not always win. He lost his confrontation with President Truman, a most costly personal risk and one that it is doubtful that he undertook without carefully weighing the reward against the possible consequences of his actions. His bid to force a victorious resolution to the Korean War was ultimately unsuccessful, and he paid for it with his career.

MacArthur did not suffer any loss easily, but as a boy, he learned to accept the possibility. In a poker hand with his grandfather, he drew four queens and bet all his chips. Arthur MacArthur took the pot with four kings and offered this bit of advice, "My dear boy, nothing is sure in this life. Everything is relative."

"There is no security in this life;
there is only opportunity."

Reflection Questions:

- How can you minimize the risk of your current strategy without reducing the potential reward?

- How are individuals who unsuccessfully undertake risk treated within your organization?

Chapter 51

Love Peace

Whether they work in business, public, nonprofit, or military realms, all leaders must deal with conflict. The causes of conflict are often outside their control, but they have choices in their responses to it. Great leaders first seek peaceful and cooperative resolutions to conflict.

MacArthur was a professional warrior, but he professed to abhor war. This attitude appears to have first emerged in WWI, during which he witnessed the wholesale slaughter firsthand. In fewer than ten months of combat, the Rainbow Division itself suffered over 14,500 casualties in the war. This was the third highest total in the American Expeditionary Force, and it represented half of the division's full authorized strength of 28,000 men.

In 1935, MacArthur had not forgotten the division's losses when he told his fellow veterans:

> *In the last 3,400 years only 268—less than 1 in 13—have been free from wars. No wonder that Plato, the wisest of all men, once exclaimed, 'Only the dead have seen the end of war!' Every reasonable man knows that war is cruel and destructive...No one desires peace as much as the soldier, for the soldier must pay the greatest penalty in war. Our Army is maintained solely for the preservation of peace...or for the restoration of peace after it has been lost by statesman or by others.*

The atomic blasts at Hiroshima and Nagasaki convinced MacArthur that war must be banned. "It is a form of mutual suicide," he said, "and I believe that the entire effort of a modern society should be concentrated on an endeavor to outlaw it."

In a 1955 speech, MacArthur explained why he had rejected war. He said:

> *Within the span of my own life I have witnessed this evolution. At the turn of the century, when I entered the Army, the target was one enemy casualty at the end of a rifle or bayonet or sword. Then came the machine gun designed to kill by the dozen. After that, the heavy artillery raining death upon the hundreds. Then the aerial bomb to strike by the thousands—followed by the atom explosion to reach the hundreds of thousands. Now, electronics and other processes of science have raised the destructive potential to encompass millions. And with restless hands we work feverishly in dark laboratories to find the means to destroy all at one blow.*
>
> *But this very triumph of scientific annihilation—this very success of invention—has destroyed the possibility of war being a medium of practical settlement of international differences.*

Article 9 in the Japanese Constitution was one way in which MacArthur put his beliefs about war and peace into action. Although the origins of the article banning war have been obscured almost from the start, the evidence suggests that the idea was introduced by MacArthur. He denied this, but he did strongly support its adoption. MacArthur also made clear that although Japan rejected war, this did not mean that the nation should be defenseless. "Article 9 is based on the highest of moral ideals," he said, "but by no sophistry of reasoning can it be interpreted as complete negation of the inalienable right of self-defense against unprovoked attack."

This is an important point. Although MacArthur proclaimed his love of peace, he understood that sometimes the price of peace made war unavoidable. It was for this reason that he condemned pacifism. In 1932, in a controversial commencement speech he gave at the University of Pittsburgh, MacArthur declared:

> *Pacifism is not the same as love of peace. It is inactive; a refusal to protect. Those who preach, by word or deed, 'peace at any price,' either do not have anything worth defending or believe nothing they have is worth defending. Such people deny their responsibilities.*
>
> *Pacific habits ensure neither peace nor immunity from national insult and aggression. Any nation that would preserve its tranquility, its rights, its independence, its self-respect, and its happiness must at all times be prepared to defend them.*

One of MacArthur's main concerns was that Americans might abandon their long history of fighting for their rights and their freedoms. He admonished us to act to uphold those values. He warned:

> *...we must not think that industry, economy, fairness, or even loyalty to our government guarantee us, forever, all the benefits which this fortunate land affords. So long as another nation, anywhere, is governed by motives not in accord with ours, our country is in possible danger from attack. We deeply believe in decency, honor, and respect for every man. Any nation which has this belief is responsible for preparing itself to defend those things against attack.*

"Could I have but a line a century hence crediting a contribution to the advance of peace, I would gladly yield every honor which has been accorded in war."

Reflection Questions:

- Do you exhaust every peaceful means of issue resolution before engaging in conflict?

- Does your organization take a cooperative approach in its relationships with suppliers, customers, and competitors?

Chapter 52

A Patriot Be

Patriotism has always been a primary consideration of civic and military leaders. These leaders swear oaths of loyalty to their nation when they assume their positions. Patriotism is no less important for today's business leaders. Many companies have expanded far beyond borders of their home country, but the benefits and protections extended by the United States remain the foundational element of their very existence.

MacArthur never took his American citizenship for granted. To him, it was the greatest of all privileges. In 1948, he told the *Los Angeles Examiner*:

> *I am an American! In that birthright is found the most precious heritage known to man. For there are embodied within it as rights, inviolate and inalienable, equality of opportunity, equality of justice, and equality of dignity. They permit men to rise from lowly birth to high station, from subordination to leadership, and infuse in the hearts and minds of all so endowed a spirituality which generates those great human forces essential to material progress—courage, energy and initiative.*

Patriotism was always a given in MacArthur's life. It was one the first values he learned as a child, and he never deviated from it. At the end of his life and near the end of his memoirs, he wrote, "The highest encomium you can still receive is to be called a patriot, if it means you love your country above all else and will place your life, if need be, at the service of your Flag."

MacArthur well understood that in a very immediate sense the American nation had been won and was maintained by sacrifice and force of arms. He supported that understanding with actions and placed the highest value on those who made sacrifices for their country. The Purple Heart is a notable example. The medal, which was our nation's first military decoration, dates back to 1782, when General George Washington had instituted the award. It was then called the Badge of Military Merit. Washington awarded it only three times, and it fell into disuse.

There were several unsuccessful attempts to revive the medal after WWI. In 1932, MacArthur led a successful effort to re-establish it in conjunction with the 200th anniversary of Washington's birth. He renamed it the Purple Heart and made its award contingent on only one condition: being wounded in the action of defending one's country. He described it as follows:

> *The Purple Heart is a unique decoration...the only one from which is entirely eliminated any application of privilege or special selection. It is conferred solely by enemy action and therefore not beholden to any other influence. It bears testimony for all time and for all eyes of a great sacrifice. It signifies the blood you have spilled in battle for our beloved country. There could be no greater honor.*

MacArthur himself received the first Purple Heart, inscribed #1 on its verso, for injuries sustained in a gas attack in WWI. More than one million Purple Heart medals have been awarded in the years since then.

Those who were wounded while fighting for their country also received MacArthur's special attention. Senator John Stennis, who was present during MacArthur's testimony at the Congressional hearings into his recall in 1951, remembered him stopping during his entrance and crossing the room "to where three or four staff members were lined up with backs to the wall. He went up to one of these gentlemen and very vigorously shook his hand...Now, later I learned that the person he went over and shook hands with was under his command and had been sent into a very dangerous area, was gravely wounded, and barely survived. The General had recognized him when he entered the room and was paying his respects to him, not only in a personal way, but for his act of valor and dedication to duty."

Like the Purple Heart, the American flag was another symbol of patriotism that MacArthur honored. In a 1949 letter, he wrote:

> *Never has there been more pressing need than now to hold that flag firmly aloft, as insidious forces both at home and abroad work unceasingly to dim its luster and destroy humanity's faith in the hallowed American traditions of personal freedom, impartial justice, and individual dignity for which it stands. The flag is a constant reminder of the blood and struggle and sacrifice upon which has been built the American way—and should inspire in us of this generation just as it did in those of the past, the will, the wisdom, and the courage to preserve and advance our sacred heritage of freedom.*

"The highest encomium you can still receive is to be called a patriot."

Reflection Questions:

- Are your actions consistent with the dictates of patriotism?

- Do your organization's policies support loyalty to nation and civic responsibility?

Sources

For those readers who want to learn more about MacArthur, we highly recommend a visit to the General Douglas MacArthur Memorial. It is a square block of downtown Norfolk, Virginia devoted to everything MacArthur.

For further reading, the three-volume biography, *The Years of MacArthur* by D. Clayton James (Professor Emeritus at Virginia Military Institute), is the definitive work. William Manchester's *American Caesar* is the best alternative for a lighter read in both length and content.

After reading a good biography of MacArthur, read his autobiography, *Reminiscences.* It is, like most memoirs, not an altogether objective version of the author's life, but there is no better way to get a sense of the cadence and rhythm of MacArthur's speech and writing styles, his approach and philosophy as a leader, his interpretation of the events in his life, and the position he saw himself occupying in the pages of history.

As MacArthur researchers, we enjoyed a wealth of sources. Our primary resource was the MacArthur Memorial's Archives and Library and the expert guidance of Archivist James Zobel. Secondarily, we drew from the memoirs of those who knew MacArthur and accounts that were published as near the actual events as possible. Finally, we drew on the many works that have been published in the decades since MacArthur's death.

Of this last category, we would be remiss if we did not acknowledge our debt to and dependence on the work of D. Clayton James. James's biography of MacArthur was our touchstone throughout the writing of this book. It was where we turned to check facts and weigh conflicting interpretations. It is an objective and monumental job of research that was 20 years in the making, and it is undeservedly out-of-print.

We chose not to footnote this book because the lessons for leaders are its main focus. As such, the book is neither meant to be a complete record of MacArthur's life and career nor a source for historians. In addition to the documents residing at the Archives, we consulted the following works:

Ambrose, Stephen E. *Duty, Honor, Country: A History of West Point* (Johns Hopkins University Press, 1966).

Appleman, Roy Edgar. *South to Naktong, North to the Yalu: June–November 1950* (Center of Military History, 1961).

Bartsch, William H. *December 8, 1941: McArthur's Pearl Harbor* (Texas A & M, 2003).

Breuer, William B. *MacArthur's Undercover War: Spies, Saboteurs, Guerrillas, and Secret Missions* (John Wiley & Sons, 1995), *Sea Wolf: The Daring Exploits of Navy Legend John D. Bulkeley* (Presidio, 1998).

Bush, Noel F. *Fallen Sun: A Report on Japan* (Appleton-Century-Crofts, 1948).

Churchill, Winston S. *Their Finest Hour: The Second World War, Vol. 2* (Mariner Books, 1986).

Chwialkowski, Paul. *In Caesar's Shadow: The Life of General Robert Eichelberger* (Greenwood, 1993).

Clark, Eugene F. *The Secrets of Inchon: The Untold Story of the Most Daring Mission of the Korean War* (Putnam, 2002).

Connaughton, Richard. *MacArthur and Defeat in the Philippines* (Overlook Press, 2001).

Cutler, Thomas J. *The Battle of Leyte Gulf: 23–26 October 1944* (HarperCollins, 1994).

Drea, Edward J. *MacArthur's ULTRA: Codebreaking and the War against Japan, 1942–1945* (University Press of Kansas, 1992).

Duffy, Bernard and Ronald H. Carpenter. *Douglas MacArthur: Warrior as Wordsmith* (Greenwood Press, 1997).

Dunn, William J. *Pacific Microphone* (Texas A & M, 1988).

Egeberg, Roger Olaf. *The General: MacArthur and the Man Called "Doc"* (Hippocrene, 1984).

Eichelberger, Robert L. and Milton McKaye. *Our Jungle Road to Tokyo* (Viking, 1951).

Eisenhower, Dwight David. *At Ease: Stories I Tell My Friends* (Doubleday, 1967).

Fehrenbach, T.R. *This Kind of War: A Study in Unpreparedness* (MacMilllan, 1963).

Finn, Richard B. *Winners in Peace: MacArthur, Yoshida, and Postwar Japan* (California, 1992).

Ganoe, William Addleman. *MacArthur Close-Up: An Unauthorized Portrait* (Vantage, 1962).

Griffith, Thomas E., Jr. *MacArthur's Airman: General George C. Kenney and the War in the Southwest Pacific* (Kansas, 1998).

Gunther, John. *The Riddle of MacArthur: Japan, Korea and the Far East* (Harper & Row, 1951).

Harsch, Joseph C. *At the Hinge of History: A Reporter's Story* (University of Georgia Press, 1993).

Higgins, Trumball. *Korea and the Fall of MacArthur: A Precis in Limited War* (Oxford University Press, 1960).

Hoyt, Edwin P. *The Bloody Road to Panmunjom* (Stein and Day, 1986).

Huff, Sid with Joe Alex Morris. *My Fifteen Years with General MacArthur* (Paperback Library, 1964).

Hunt, Frazier. *The Untold Story of Douglas MacArthur* (Devin-Adair, 1954).

James, D. Clayton. *Refighting the Last War: Command and Crisis in Korea 1950–1953* (Free Press, 1993), *A Time for Giants: The Politics of the American High Command in World War II* (Watts, 1987), *The Years of MacArthur, 1880–1941, Volume I* (Houghton Mifflin, 1970), *The Years of MacArthur, 1941–1945, Volume II* (Houghton Mifflin, 1975), *The Years of MacArthur, Triumph & Disaster 1945–1964, Volume III* (Houghton Mifflin, 1985).

Kelley, Frank and Cornelius Ryan. *MacArthur: Man of Action* (Doubleday, 1950).

Kenney, George C. *General Kenney Reports: A Personal History of the Pacific War* (Air Force History and Museums, 1997), *The MacArthur I Know* (Duell, Sloan and Pearce, 1951).

Langley, Michael. *Inchon Landing: MacArthur's Last Triumph* (Times Books, 1979).

Lauterbach, Richard E. *Danger from the East* (Harper, 1947).

Long, Gavin. *MacArthur: His Life and Battles* (Combined Publishing, 1969).

Lynn, John A. *Battle: A History of Combat and Culture* (Westview, 2003).

MacArthur, Douglas and Frank C. Waldrop, editor. *MacArthur On War* (Duell, Sloan and Pearce, 1942).

MacArthur, Douglas. *Reminiscences* (McGraw-Hill, 1964).

MacArthur, Douglas, as prepared by His General Staff. *Reports of General MacArthur: The Campaigns of MacArthur in the Pacific, Volume I* (Center of Military History, 1994), *Reports of General MacArthur: MacArthur in Japan: The Occupation: Military Phase, Volume I Supplement* (Center of Military History, 1994).

MacArthur, Douglas and John M. Pratt, editor. *Revitalizing a Nation* (Heritage Foundation, 1952).

MacArthur, Douglas and Vorin E. Whan, Jr., editor. *A Soldier Speaks: Public Papers and Speeches of General of the Army Douglas MacArthur* (Praeger, 1965).

McCullough, David. *Truman* (Simon & Schuster, 1992).

Manchester, William. *American Caesar: Douglas MacArthur 1880–1964* (Little, Brown, 1978).

Miller, John J. *CARTWHEEL: The Reduction of Rabaul* (Center of Military History, 1989).

Milner, Samuel. *Victory in Papua* (Center of Military History, 1989).

Morton, Louis. *The Fall of the Philippines* (Center of Military History, United States Army, 1953).

Perret, Geoffrey. *Old Soldiers Never Die: The Life of Douglas MacArthur* (Random House, 1996).

Phillips, Cabell. *The Truman Presidency: The History of a Triumphant Succession* (Macmillan Company, 1966).

Prefer, Nathan. *MacArthur's New Guinea Campaign: March–August 1944* (Combined Publishing, 1995).

Puryear, Edgar F., Jr. *19 Stars: A Study in Military Character and Leadership* (Presidio Press, 1994).

Rasor, Eugene. *General Douglas MacArthur 1880–1964: Historiography and Annotated Bibliography* (Greenwood, 1994).

Rees, David. *Korea: The Limited War* (Penguin, 1970).

Rhodes, Weldon E. *Flying MacArthur to Victory* (Texas A&M, 1987).

Rogers, Paul P. *The Bitter Years: MacArthur and Sutherland* (Praeger, 1990), *The Good Years: MacArthur and Sutherland* (Praeger, 1990).

Rovere, Richard H. and Arthur M. Schlesinger, Jr. *The General and the President: And the Future of American Foreign Policy* (Farrar, Straus & Young, 1951).

Schaller, Michael. *The American Occupation of Japan: the Origins of the Cold War in Asia* (Oxford, 1985), *Douglas MacArthur: The Far Eastern General* (Oxford, 1989).

Shortal, John F. *Forged By Fire: Robert L. Eichelberger and the Pacific War* (University of South Carolina Press, 1987).

Sides, Hampton. *Ghost Soldiers: The Epic Account of WWII's Greatest Rescue Mission* (Anchor Books, 2002).

Snyder, Joe. *Para(graph) Trooper for MacArthur* (Leathers Publishing, 1997).

Truman, Harry S. *Memoirs of Harry S. Truman: 1946–52 Years of Trial and Hope* (Smithmark, 1996).

Truman, Harry S. and Margaret Truman, editor. *Where the Buck Stops: The Personal and Private Writings of Harry S. Truman* (Warner Books, 1990).

United States Senate. *Testimony of General Douglas MacArthur Before the Armed Services and Foreign Relations Committees of the United States Senate, 82nd Congress, First Session, May 3–5, 1951* (Hour-Glass Publishers, 1966).

Valley, David J. *Gaijin Shogun: General Douglas A. MacArthur Stepfather of Postwar Japan 1945–1951* (Sektor Co., 2000).

Weinberger, Caspar W. and Gretchen Roberts. *In the Arena: A Memoir of the 20th Century* (Regnery, 2001).

Weintraub, Stanley. *MacArthur's War: Korea and the Undoing of an American Hero* Touchstone, 2000).

Whitney, Courtney. *MacArthur: His Rendezvous with Destiny* (Knopf, 1956).

Willoughby, Charles A. and John Chamberlain. *MacArthur 1941–1951* (McGraw-Hill, 1954).

The MacArthur Memorial and the General Douglas MacArthur Foundation

The MacArthur Memorial dates to 1961, when General Douglas MacArthur executed a deed of gift in which he gave the City of Norfolk all his trophies, medals, prizes, decorations, uniforms, flags, swords, battle souvenirs, personal papers, documents, records, and other personal memorabilia. These items now reside in the four buildings that comprise the Memorial, which is located in MacArthur Square in downtown Norfolk, Virginia.

The museum proper is housed in Norfolk's historic 1850 City Hall. The monumental rotunda serves as General and Mrs. MacArthur's final resting place, where they are surrounded by inscriptions, banners, and flags heralding the general's long and glorious career. The extensive collection of military and personal artifacts allows visitors to discover the compelling story of General of the Army Douglas MacArthur and the millions of American men and women who served our nation during the Civil War, Indian Wars, Spanish American War, World War I, World War II, the Occupation of Japan, and the Korean War.

The Museum's displays are housed in nine permanent and two changing exhibit galleries. The treasures on view include 19th and 20th century medals, flags, paintings, weapons, and equipment. Philippine, Japanese, Korean, and Chinese art objects, including Imari, Kutani, and Satsuma porcelain, are also displayed. Included throughout the museum are personal artifacts belonging to General Douglas MacArthur and his family. Among these artifacts are the General's trademark military cap, corncob pipe, and sunglasses.

The Jean MacArthur Research Center (named after the General's widow) houses the library and archives, an education wing, and the administrative offices of the MacArthur Memorial and the General Douglas MacArthur Foundation. The non-lending reference and research library contains General MacArthur's original collection of 5,000 volumes, and is augmented by gifts and purchases of books concerning the General, his times, and his associates. The archives hold some 2 million documents, 90,000 photographs, 150 photograph albums, and 250 motion picture films, in addition to sound recordings, newspapers, rare books, scrapbooks, and microfilms.

General MacArthur's correspondence and papers are both personal and official; they include his private correspondence as well as his headquarters' official files of letters, reports, photographs, messages, memoranda, and orders. Of particular interest to researchers have been the documents on the General's tenure as Philippine Military Advisor; the unique materials on the first months of the war in the Philippines, 1941–1942; WWII; the occupation and rehabilitation of Japan; the Korean War; the message files of 1941–1951; the photographic collection; and the General's private correspondence.

The MacArthur Memorial's education program provides visitors with a view of history and their heritage based on the life and times of General MacArthur and the men and women who have served in the United States Armed Forces. The education department conducts programs for preschool through adult, in many subjects relating to the period 1861–1964. These programs contain films, audiotapes, photographs, and historical information. While at the MacArthur Memorial, the visitors receive orientation in the chosen program (films, round-table discussions, maps, hands-on artifacts), tour the museum exhibits, and then perform an activity that helps them use the study of history in their own lives. Teacher in-service programs are available on request. Special conferences and symposia are conducted periodically.

Admission to the Macarthur Memorial is free.

The General Douglas MacArthur Foundation was established in 1962 to commemorate the life and achievements of General Douglas MacArthur, particularly as they relate to his credo "Duty, Honor, Country" and its relevance to future generations of Americans. The Foundation is a nonprofit corporation chartered in the Commonwealth of Virginia.

The Foundation supports many programs to meet its goals. First, and foremost is the support of the Memorial. Over the years, it has provided funding for the larger-than-life bronze statue of the general; and for the building of of the Jean MacArthur Research Center, theater, gift shop, and the latest upgrades to the permanent exhibits in the Memorial.

The Foundation also promotes research, study, and publications to make known the achievements of General MacArthur. Projects are undertaken with outside agencies such as the Department of Defense, other museums, veterans' organizations, and educational institutions. Special events commemorating General MacArthur are conducted on historic dates. Annual awards for excellence are presented for individual leadership and achievement, and historical scholarship.

The Foundation receives funds from memberships in the MacArthur Committee, donations from visitors to the Memorial, profits from the gift shop, and the largest portion from an endowment fund. Membership in the MacArthur Committee plays an important role in keeping alive MacArthur's ideals. Contributions are tax-deductible to the full extent of the law. Members receive a subscription to *The MacArthur Report* newsletter and a 10% discount at the MacArthur Memorial Gift Shop. Membership levels include:

National Member: $25 or $50
Five Star Member: $100 to $999
MacArthur One Thousand Member: $1,000
Corporate Member: $250, $500, $1,000

If you want to become a member of the MacArthur Committee, please contact the MacArthur Memorial for a membership enrollment card. Or you can send your check or MasterCard/VISA information (including expiration date) to:

The General Douglas MacArthur Foundation
MacArthur Square
Norfolk, VA 23510
Phone (757) 441–2968
FAX (757) 441–5389
Web page: www.macarthurmemorial.org

Index

A

D

E

L

M

Q-R

S

T

X-Z